Teaching Creative Writing

A Teaching Handbook with Weekly Lesson Plans

Plus an Abundance of Writing Ideas

by

Valerie Hockert, PhD

Second Edition

Valerie Hockert
realitytodayforum@gmail.com

Copyright: © 2014, 2012 by Reality Today Forum, Inc. All rights reserved

No part of this document may be reproduced or transmitted in any form or by any means, electronic, mechanical, photocopying, recording, or otherwise, without prior written permission of author.

About the Author

Valerie Hockert, PhD has written over 50 published books, over 150 articles, and has worked as a publisher and editor. She is also is a college professor, teaching English, composition, writing, journalism, literature, and humanities.

Introduction

Often I find that people are interested in writing, but don't know how to get started or how to get their "creative juices" flowing. While teaching creative writing courses in a local college, I experimented with various methods and obtained some interesting results. I designed the class to help the student get his/her "creative juices" flowing.

I presented to the students many sources for ideas, exercises to get them started, rewriting exercises, and how to avoid writer's block. I designed various creative writing exercises, including different types of paragraph development, and stories to rewrite, all designed to get their "creative juices" flowing.

The members of the classes I taught represented various age levels--from 18 to 60--and were of various writing levels. Since this was the case, I found that the exercises I used (included in this book) had various results, but nevertheless were beneficial to most students.

You will be able to use this book as a 16-week course, or can combine some lessons to fit a shorter course plan.

Table of Contents

Lesson One 7

    Introductions 7

Lesson Two 9

    Where and How to Get Ideas 9

Lesson Three 21

    Getting Many Writing Ideas from One Trip 21

Lesson Four 25

    Writing Stories from Dreams 25

Lesson Five 34

    Producing Ideas through Questions 34

Lesson Six 54

    Various Ways of Developing a Paragraph 54

Lesson Seven 60

    Rewriting a Story 60

Lesson Eight 68

    Story Rewrite 68

Lesson Nine 90

    Making Your Writing Stand Out From the Crowd
    90

Lesson Ten 95

    Proper Formatting & Redundancy 95

Lesson Eleven 102

  Avoiding Common Errors 102

Lesson Twelve 105

  Using Starter Sentences 105

Lesson Thirteen 107

  Good Writing 107

Lesson Fourteen 118

  Creative Writing Exercises 118

Lesson Fifteen 121

  More Writing Exercises 121

Lesson Sixteen 125

  Current Events 125

Feedback for Classmates 127

Stories About Us 128

365 Writing Ideas 132

Conclusion 162

Lesson One

Introductions

Introductions: First introduce yourself, and tell of your past writing experiences, educational background, and any other writing-related experience. Then have each student in turn, introduce himself/herself. Instruct them to say their name, why they are taking the class, their interest in writing, and any writing experience.

You may discover that most of the students may seem to find writing an outlet and expression for emotions and frustrations.

After the introductions, students will most likely be anxious to start writing and to analyze their writing ability, so begin with the basic writing exercise below.

First Basic Exercise: Choose a chair in the room for them to write about. Instruct them to use their imagination and write about anything connected with the chair. For example: how it got there, the chair as an antique, or the chair as a childhood favorite. Have students write a paragraph of at least five sentences; give them 15 minutes to complete the assignment. Then have each student read his/her paragraph aloud, and invite comments from the other students. Since this is a first exercise, you may find that your students may be quite conservative in their comments, as well as in their writing.

Second Basic Exercise: Ask the students to write a paragraph describing "where they'd like to live happily ever after." For example: someplace where the weather is nice, a favorite vacation spot, at home, or even in outer space. Again, have the students read them aloud. This time you may find that your students are a little more liberal in their comments, as well as in their writing.

Some students may think that at this point that they have had enough writing and sharing for one class session, so for the rest of the class time, you can talk of where they can get ideas to write about. As you go through the list, invite comments from your students.

Lesson Two

Where and How to Get Ideas

Where and how to get ideas is important for a writer's success, because without new and interesting ideas, it's difficult to spark a reader's interest.

Here are some places to look for fresh ideas:

Yourself. A special job, a unique personal experience you've had, special interests, hobbies or places you've been, are all good sources for ideas.

Other People. Their special skills, hobbies, how problems can be solved, or an outstanding achievement, can be great topics to write on.

Family. Your family may be a great source for ideas. Many of you may have families that you could write soap operas on. Articles on alternative lifestyles, coping with additions, young people's sense of entitlement, teaching children to be independent, blended families, suicide within the family--these are all great topics to write on.

TV. Soap operas, series shows, and sitcoms are a great source for ideas and characterizations. Just watching one episode can help; shows such as: Dallas, Mike & Molly, The Big Bang Theory. You can learn what subjects are of great social concern, and how people really do handle these difficult situations, as well as actual related dialogue.

Movies. Movies can be a great source, too. Even though many movies are fiction, watching movies can give one ideas that can help portray a fantasy world.

Work. Many people have work situations, or work with people who have great accomplishments and successes, or work with very unusual people. These people can also be great sources for stories, articles, and books.

Newspapers. There are many ideas that can surface by reading news stories. A follow-up could be written, or perhaps you could present the other side of the issue.

Many times when reading through a newspaper, you may think that the writer or reporter didn't say anything about_____. You could probably present that side of the issue. You could also write follow-ups to many stories. For example: a house fire. We always hear about the fire, but what happens to the occupants six months later? How do they piece their lives back together? A follow-up could be written on that, and would be a great human interest story.

There have been stories in the news where someone was shot, claiming it was self-defense, and have created quite a debatable opinion. These various opinions could be explored with examples to support them.

Magazines. After reading an article, you may want to write a different viewpoint on the topic. Or write about the topic with a different slant for another market. When you read various articles, you may think that the article could be presented in a different way. You could write that.

Just reading through other magazines of course, can give one ideas for other writing.

Advertisements. Signs, billboards, television, radio, and printed ads may inspire an idea for a story. Perhaps the background of the business or item being advertised could be a good story.

Signs. Check out those flashing signs with the flashing message that you see at shopping centers or banks. The ones at banks are of particular interest because many times they advertise interest rates for a loan or a money market, yet the message flashes by so fast that one is almost off the road turning one's neck to read the message. These messages seem to flash at a third-grade reading level. Yet, who with only a third-grade reading level would be interested in what interest rates one can get on the money market? This could make for an interesting piece, first doing some research to discover what speed these messages actually flash at, and then how the speed is determined. Another perspective could be from an advertising standpoint—are these signs a waste of money?

Billboards. These can inspire ideas for different pieces of writing. You could write from an artistic viewpoint, a grammatical viewpoint, or any other viewpoint that you choose. An example is that there seems to be a trend to the two-color billboard from the multi-color one. An essay could be written from an artistic standpoint. Then there were the Kemps cows: remember all the different types of cows? That could inspire an idea for a children's story! Then there are billboards that don't make any sense (like one that says a revolutionary event is about to happen! What event?. Billboards with misspellings!--now there's an idea from a grammatical viewpoint. If you travel to Florida or southern Texas, you may see many billboards with misspelled words.

Television Ads. Remember the Blue Cross ad with the man who was dancing and the slogan was "move that body"? There were some follow-up stories on that commercial and what was behind it. (If you remember, it gave the man in the commercial some publicity). You could select a particular commercial and write what's behind it. (My favorite commercial is _____).

NOTE: Tell the students about your favorite commercial. There are a lot of interesting commercials--like those on the newest anti-wrinkle creams. What makes the viewer go out and purchase the product? What drives a consumer to purchase any product?

Radio. Again, you can write about what's behind the ad.

Printed Ads. This can inspire an idea to write a history on a particular business.

Old Letters. Rereading old letters can inspire ideas about: old friends, events, travel, and entertainment.

Scrapbooks. Looking through a scrapbook (or scrap-box, or junk drawer) at memorabilia, can bring back memories which can be great topics to write on--memories of various events, travel, entertainment, romance, and more.

You can also write about the great new past time of "scrapbooking."

Snapshots. Looking at old snapshots can inspire ideas about the person or persons in the snapshot, background, or foreground. Try looking at an old snapshot through a magnifying glass--you may find something of interest to write on that you had forgotten about, or may find of interest someone's expression. Or look at a family portrait, perhaps write a story on the family members in the portrait who pretend to be happy and get along, when they aren't and don't.

Conversations Overheard in a Restaurant. Family restaurants are great sources for ideas, as you can hear what people are talking about all around you. This is a great source for dialogue. Many people meet at family restaurants for a business meeting, or to socialize. You can usually hear what's going on at every table--people who are having affairs, people who haven't seen each other for a long time, someone's having a fight, an elderly couple analyzing every entree on the menu.... You may even see people at family restaurants, sitting by themselves and taking notes, perhaps writing down bits of conversations.

State Fairs. A great source for ideas and for characterizations, as it seems that people come from all over for this event. It's a great place to watch people.

Art Festivals. You can see a lot of eccentric people at these events.

Airports. Airports are great. If you're traveling, the person sitting next to you may be an interesting source for ideas. Also, when you are waiting for someone, you may find a lot of interesting people from different geographic locations. Then there's the person who reveals too much information while talking on his/her cell phone. Or the person who is "checking out" another person.

Concerts and Other Big Events. Particularly check out those events that you would have to get to in plenty of time to get a parking spot, a good seat, or a place in line. I'm sure that all of you have arrived at an event early, and while waiting for the event to happen or begin, you elbow the person next to you, because what you hear is so entertaining, you want to listen and want your companion to listen too. This is a great way to get actual dialogue.

Shopping Malls. Listen to conversations between other people as they are shopping, and passing through the mall. It's a great source for ideas, characterizations, and dialogue. Try going shopping when there aren't so many people around, as you may be more aware of things that go on around you. You may be in a dressing room and hear people in adjoining dressing rooms saying: "This isn't right," "This doesn't fit," "Well I guess we just have to go back to work and earn some money, we can't spend any here." This could conjure ideas about the way clothes fit today, or how manufacturers size clothing; or shopping on lunch hours....

NOTE: During a department store's big sale, a couple came in to shop, and the husband wanted a Twins souvenir mug. The author portrayed the husband as a wimpy type, and the wife as an overpowering type. The wife did not want the husband to have the mug. She said "it collects dust." There were a lot of people around, and instead of them getting anxious and frustrated, the people were cheering on the husband. He eventually got his mug. The wife was outnumbered. A writer could sell a story like this to the department store, or to a publication published by the mall (that advertises the mall's various stores. A story like this would make people want to go to the next sale, and is great publicity for the store.

I'm sure that all of us at some time or other have been shopping and have come across a situation that is just so humorous that you just "have to" stand around and watch, and you forget (or no longer care) that you were in a hurry. This can be worth writing about.

Many times you see scenarios between parents and teenage children. This can be interesting, as you could do comparisons, like why do some teenagers think that they have to wear designer jeans, or certain brands, and others don't? Why isn't a less expensive brand just as good? Or write a comparison on how it was different when you grew up. Or perhaps just write an article on the significance of having a certain brand item, or an article on why some kids just don't care. Or do some kids decide they don't care because they just plain can't afford it? Or why do some parents not want these things for their kids?

Bars. Do you ever notice the stories some people tell in bars? Write these stories, or use elements of these characters or bits of their dialogue in your writing.

Buses. The bus lines transport a variety of people--great for characterizations and dialogue.

Reunions. Family reunions, class reunions, and other reunions, can give you ideas on: family background, historical pieces, someone's success or failure, how someone changed, and many other ideas.

Family Reunions. You can get an idea at a family reunion by talking to some elderly relatives. Perhaps do some research and write a love story connected with your grandparents moving from overseas.

NOTE: *When you are doing something set in a different county, you should try to visit that country and/or do some extensive geographical or historical research in the library or online.*

A family history may be nice to write before it is forgotten by younger generations.

Then there's the black sheep in the family-- why is this person different from everybody else? The generation gap is a good topic, or young people's sense of entitlement. Or there may be a family member who has gone through a traumatic experience--how did he/she survive it?

Class Reunions. The guy you thought was "Mr. Wonderful" is now fat and bald, and the one who was the "nerd" now has the great job, is good-looking and drives the nice car. Then there are those who never change. Or you could write on parallels. For example: the guy in your graduating class from high school who was in the most trouble, still is,--he's a stockbroker on Wall Street. Perhaps those who were in the most trouble (not drugs and alcohol, but the pranksters--are the most successful in business today, as they are more willing to take a risk. Is this true? Do some research.

Travel. Not only your own travel experiences, but other people's travel experiences are good sources for ideas. You don't necessarily have to travel far. For example: when traveling from the north to the south, you may discover malls that use different means of entertainment (example: skating rinks, amusement parks). You may also discover things that are standard in a house that aren't standard where you live—perhaps intercom systems, or ceiling fans.

Now don't overlook the foreigner who is here for a visit, and his/her reactions to surroundings here. For example: the foreigner who is shopping, and his/her amazement at some of the merchandise sold here in our country, can be remarkable and worth writing about. Their reactions to our way of living, or our housing, is of equal interest. For example: having a new friend from a fighting country over to your home where there are sliding glass doors and big picture windows, may prompt a response that having all that glass is not safe, the fear being that someone could come up to the house and shoot. After all, he/she may be used to living under terrorist conditions, and having to hide under furniture, and stayed away from windows and glass. Yet we may sit in front of our sliding glass doors and don't even pull the blinds! You can imagine the terror this visitor would experience if he/she were to enter a newer house with much glass and/or solar panels, or a newer office building built with a lot of glass.

Vacation Spots. Campgrounds are great places to gather characterizations, dialogue, and tales from other people. You also could be inspired to write on the outdoors, animals, and nature.

Other "tourist trap" vacation spots (for example: Disney World, a popular resort) can be great spots as--you guessed it--a lot of people go there, and yes!--it's a great source for characterizations and dialogue.

Children. Small children are very candid with their opinions (unless they live under abusive conditions which can make them afraid to speak). They can be a great source for ideas for children's stories, or stories on parenting.

Teenagers. We read a lot of the "terrible teenager." How about some writing on the good teenager? It may boost the morale of teenagers to know they aren't "weird" when they're good. Or how do teenagers become so bad? Is it the parents' fault? Does the apple not fall far from the tree?

Retired People. This is a great source for topics on coping with retirement and/or each other, and other family members. Also, what risks are there for retired people—economic, social, and safety?

Old People. Old people many times have stored a wealth of information. Memoirs, historical pieces, human interest pieces, and other ideas can be inspired by old people. Of particular interest are those old people who are getting to the point of senility, where they start to ramble on and on. It's a good idea to tape these conversations, in case you'd like to refer to them later, when the elderly person passes on.

Divorce. We all read and hear about the divorced father who doesn't make his child support payments, or the divorced mother who lives on welfare. What about the less typical divorces where the reverse is true, or where the father has custody, or other unusual situations?

Animals. Pets and other animals are a great source for ideas on animal stories, children's stories, and adventure stories.

Nature. Nature can be a great inspiration. A walk through the woods not only can help to clear your mind, but fill your mind with ideas to write on.

Feelings. Using feelings such as love, depression, fear, and anxiety can help create a great emotional-packed piece of writing.

Dreams. An excellent source, particularly for fiction stories, is dreams. You can sometimes make yourself have dreams by changing sleeping place, as it can cause dreams to happen more spontaneously. Also sleeping longer than usual can cause dreams to occur, as most dreams occur in the lighter stages of sleep before awakening.

***

Assignment:

Your students should now have many ideas to write on. Have them write a short story of one of the above ideas.

Lesson Three

Getting Many Writing Ideas from One Trip

What should I write about? There are so many things that I have seen and done--which should I choose? Can I get more than one article out of this trip? Are these questions you ask yourself after having traveled?

I had visited the South Pacific on assignment by a cruise ship company, and my job was to write an article featuring the cruise ship, and to take photos to illustrate the article. I had never been to the South Pacific before, so many things appeared awesome to me, and many things were different, compared to what us North Americans are used to.

The cruise, of course, was wonderful--top notch, five-star--couldn't be better. Food was great, service was great, activities offered were great, accommodations were great. However, I stayed a couple extra days in Tahiti, and saw a lot more-- including heavy tropical rains. It's very interesting that they can survive these rains under thatched roofs. It makes one wonder how the roofs are constructed so they don't collapse. Also, like in other tourist areas, the hotels have open, breezy restaurants, with no windows. How come these aren't destroyed? At home it seems as if any significant amount of rain does some damage--everything from flooding, to leakage, to mildew, to mosquitoes. But they--and their housing--survive.

How do they dress? Now this is definitely "pareo land." Instead of the usual t-shirt vendors, there are *pareo venders.* All the native women wear pareos--and most all the men. Men wear theirs usually as skirts, although another way is to tie them like a diaper. Women wear the pareos in many different ways; it was great fun trying to get one tied properly for a Polynesian barbecue; however, you can find books in gift shops on how to tie the pareo. Pareos come in many prints and fabrics--mostly brightly colored, and mostly of a cotton or rayon type. And amazingly enough, we found that they are quite comfortable.

Every day was an adventure; going horseback riding (walking, trotting, and galloping down the beach) in Huahine; then on a river cruise in Raiatea; a safari in Bora Bora, and a bus tour in Moorea. All of these activities were adventures in themselves. Then, of course, was the usual sightseeing, shopping, and going to the beach.

Some days, even though the sun barely *poked* through, I ended up with a very dark tan. This conjured up ideas of how some Americans have warped ideas of how much sun they need to get tan. And it enabled me to participate in other activities.

I like a good beer, and found it interesting that most places offered only three kinds--Hinano (a local Tahitian beer), Heineken, and Budweiser.

I met many people--the greatest percentage being from Europe. These people were very interested in the educational aspects of the tour--more so than many of the Americans that we met. I wondered how much they paid for their trips as compared to what an American would pay--more or less? While talking to the various tourists that I met, we found that many of them had various expectations, and various reasons for taking this particular vacation.

I flew on a foreign airline out of Los Angeles, which treated its passengers quite differently from any domestic airline I have been on.

The language spoken in the South Pacific is mostly native, or French. I vowed that when I return (hopefully in another year or so) that I will have taken at least one French class so I can better converse with the natives, as most of the natives speak little English. Yet they are very hospitable, and welcome strangers.

The colors in the sea and foliage in the South Pacific are very different from the Caribbean, of which I am more familiar *with*. Only good color photos can reveal the beauty—and, of course, seeing it firsthand.

Needless to say, the food was extraordinary--on the cruise, as well as in the islands--and very low fat, and healthy. Perhaps we should all learn to cook like these natives. And many, many fruits grow wild. The pineapple was the best and most yellow and sweet pineapple I have ever had; the bananas were about half the size of our bananas but very, very sweet; grapefruit was of a light green color.

Now, with this brief description of this trip, you can see that there are many additional writing ideas: the cruise ship, housing, dress, adventurous activities, tanning, beer, educational aspects, tourists, foreign airlines, language barriers, colors, and food.

Where have *you* been lately? Try to make a list of at least ten different topics that you could write about from your experiences to that destination.

***

Assignments:
1) Write two or three paragraphs describing your closet. (This one usually results in a wide variety of responses.)
2) Write a short story (1-2 pages) on preparing a romantic dinner.
3) Write a short story (1-2 pages) on what you think the ideal sales clerk should be like.

Lesson Four

Writing Stories from Dreams

Discuss the assignment(s) that you gave the students at the end of the last class. You may even want to select a few to read aloud, or ask for volunteers to read theirs.

Dreams

Remind the students that dreams are a great source for fiction stories. Ask if anyone has one they would like to share (in good taste, of course, so as not to offend anyone).

NOTE: I get many of my ideas for fiction stories from dreams. I have also written, and have published, a couple children's stories which were based on re-occurring nightmares I had as a child, one which is entitled "Ding! Dong! The Witch is Dead!" I would read this to my classes, and then we would discuss it. I discovered that it produced various responses ranging from dreams about witches, to dreams about running away, to what the dream could possibly mean.

***

Ding! Dong! The Witch is Dead!

When I was a small child I always liked to walk outside in the puddles after a big summer rain.

One day, while running barefoot through the rain puddles in the gutter along the street, I came to the corner where there was a manhole. I noticed the cover was loose. Temptation got the best of me, and forced me to lift the cover up and move it aside. It took all of my strength, but I made it!

What could be down there, I wondered. I bent over to look inside, but to my disappointment, there was nothing--only dark!

Thinking I'd be a good girl, and since I satisfied my curiosity, I got up to put the cover back. I tripped! The next thing I knew I was falling down the manhole through the dark.

I closed my eyes, as I was scared. I landed with a thud, on my behind. Ouch! With my eyes still closed, I felt around me. There was something soft. I opened my eyes. I was sitting on grass. Somebody's yard. I looked around and saw that I was in Jeannie's yard. Their house is right on the corner of the block, by the manhole.

How could this be? I must have dreamt that I fell!

I'll go see if Jeannie is home. Maybe she can tell me what happened, as she is several years older than me and much wiser. I went to the door, and knocked--no one was home. Wait--I hear a lawn mower. It's her dad in the back mowing the lawn. I won't ask him, though, because he has a wooden leg, and he would probably think I was silly--and what if he would kick me? No--I'll go find someone else.

Oh, my bottom hurts from the fall. I guess I'll go home. Maybe mommy can make it feel better.

Wait--I'll stop and see if Paul is home. He lives next door to Jeannie. I go to the door and ring the doorbell. A strange woman answers. Paul doesn't live here anymore, she said. How strange! When did he move? And why didn't I know that he did? Where was I?

There's one more house yet before I get to mine. Guess I'll stop there and see if Lisa is home. I want somebody to play with. After all, it's not supper time for a while yet.

Knock, knock! An old man comes to the door. Maybe he is Lisa's grandpa. No, he says, he's never heard of this Lisa character.

This is getting scary! *I want my mommy!* I run home. My door is locked. I ring the doorbell. No one answers. I sit on the steps and think. That's funny, my mommy never locks the door unless she's going someplace. And she wouldn't leave me all alone. And what about my little sisters and brother? Where are they? And where is my older brother? Daddy is at work. But where is mommy?

"Can I help you little girl?" asks a voice. I locate the voice. It belongs to a strange woman in my house. "I want my mommy. Who are you? What are you doing here?" I ask. I open the door and try to push my way in.

She puts her arms out and stops me. She asks me what I want. I tell her that I want my mommy. She says this is her house and my mommy is not here. She doesn't know my mommy. "She's here. She's here," I cry. The strange woman insists she's not, pushes me outside and leaves me on the steps, crying.

What is going on? I am scared!

I know. Maybe the *witch* that lives behind Jeannie's house knows what is going on. I'll go see. I quickly collect all my bravery and hurry on.

I get to the *witch's* house. There's a strange woman in her yard raking leaves.

"The *witch* is not home, little girl," she says. "But I'm here! Ha! Ha! Ha! Ha! Ha! Ha! Ha!" Such a strange laugh.

I swallow hard and squeak. "What's happening to me?"

"You fell down the manhole. Down here is just like up there, except there are different people down here."

"I want my mommy." I sit down on the grass and cry. Through my tears I see that she has a ladder lying near the hedge near where she stands. I'm thinking, if I can get the ladder, I can put it by the manhole on the corner by Jeannie's house and get back up. And what luck! It's one of those ladders that get longer! An extension ladder.

Again, I gather all the courage I have and ask, "Could I borrow your ladder, please?"

"To get back up there? Don't be silly. You're here to stay!"

I get up and run to the ladder and try to drag it off. She stops me. We fight over the ladder, each trying to get it away from each other. The ladder hits her on the head. Oh, no! She falls to the ground! I stand there, holding the ladder. I think she's dead! Oh, no! I killed her! What should I do? Call the cops? How would I explain how I got here? And maybe they aren't even real cops!

I grab the ladder and run as fast as I can. It's heavy. I finally get to the corner of Jeannie's house. I stand the ladder up. It catches on something up there in the dark. But it feels pretty sturdy. I'd better try it now or never.

I run up the ladder, through the dark. "Mommy, mommy," I'm crying. I get to the top. There's Jeannie, Paul, Lisa, and my older brother jumping rope and singing, "Ding! Dong! The *Witch* is Dead!"

No time to stop and play now. I need to see my mommy. I run home where I know I am safe.

***

This story was also rewritten later, and published again, this time under the title "Sarah Made the Witch Vanish!"

***

Sarah Made the Witch Vanish!

"Don't go near that manhole, unless you want the WITCH to get you," said older brother Tony." "You better watch it, or the WITCH will come by and push you in," Tony added.

Sarah ignored Tony—for the most part—until that fateful day when Sarah was running barefoot through the rain puddles in the gutter along the street.

Look! The cover is loose! Sarah looked around, and seeing no one was looking, she lifted the cover up and moved it aside. It was heavy! Sarah looked inside. Only dark!

When Sarah got up to put the cover back, she tripped. Her foot was caught in the hole. Oh, no! Sarah was falling! Through a dark, dark tunnel. It seemed like Sarah was falling forever. Would it ever end? Will Sarah ever stop falling?

Sarah closed her eyes. "I'm scared!" Sarah cried. Plop! Sarah landed on her behind! Ouch! Sarah didn't know if she should open her eyes. Sarah felt something soft around her.

Sarah then opened her eyes, and discovered she was sitting on grass! And it wasn't dark anymore. She thought it looked like her friend Jeannie's yard. How could this happen? Sarah went to the door and knocked. No one was home.

Ouch! Sarah's bottom hurt from the fall. Maybe mommy can make it feel better.

Sarah started home, but decided to stop and see if Paul was home. Paul is Sarah's brother's best friend. And he has a new bicycle. He lives next door to Jeannie. A woman answers the door. That's funny. Paul's mother always answers the door. Or Paul does.

"Paul doesn't live here anymore," she said. Huh? When did he move? And why didn't Sarah know that he did? Sarah couldn't ask her though, because she slammed the door in her face.

Maybe Sarah can play with Lisa. Sarah wanted somebody to play with.

An old man with a big white beard came to the door. Maybe he is Lisa's grandpa, Sarah thought, although she had never seen Lisa's grandpa before. No, he says, he's never heard of this Lisa character. Character? Lisa's not a character. She's a girl!

This is getting scary! Sarah cries "I WANT MY MOMMY!" Sarah runs home. The door is locked. Sarah rings the doorbell. No one answers. Sarah sits on the steps. My mommy never locks the door unless she's going someplace. She wouldn't leave without telling me. And she wouldn't leave me all alone. And what about my little sisters? Where are they? And where is Tony? Daddy is at work. But where is mommy? Sarah cried and cried.

"Can I help you little girl?" asks a woman's voice.

"I want my mommy. Who are you? What are you doing in my house?" Sarah asked. Sarah opened the door and tried to push her way in.

This woman pushes Sarah outside, and leaves her on the steps crying.

Sarah decides she is going to find the WITCH, because Tony says the WITCH can cast spells and make weird things happen. Maybe that's what she did—cast a spell on Sarah. Maybe she's not a really bad WITCH though. Maybe she can help Sarah.

HA! HA! HA! HA! HA! HA!" laughs the WITCH when she sees Sarah.

What's happening to me?" cries Sarah.

"You fell down the manhole. Down here we don't like little kids. There are just WITCHES like me."

"Where's my mommy? I want my mommy!" Sarah sat down on the grass and cried. Through Sarah's tears she could see a ladder lying near the hedge, where the WITCH was standing.

But how does Sarah get the ladder? It's so heavy. How does Sarah dare ask for it? Sarah thinks for a minute and wipes her eyes. Tony would say, "I dare you."

Sarah suddenly gets braver and asks, "Could Sarah borrow your ladder? Please?"

"To get back up there? Don't be silly."

Sarah runs for the ladder. The WITCH grabs Sarah's arm. They fight over the ladder. The ladder hits the WITCH. She falls to the ground. She doesn't get up. She doesn't move. Then—she vanishes!

Sarah starts running away from the WITCH and the WITCH'S house. She then finds a staircase. She runs up as fast as she can. It gets dark as Sarah runs up the staircase. Then Sarah feels a wind.

Sarah lands with a thud on her bottom. Sarah sits for a minute, then opens one eye first, then the other eye. Sarah looks around. She was on her street. And there was Jeannie, Paul, Lisa and Tony, playing jump rope.

"Sarah! Where were you? It's your turn to jump!" yells Tony.

***

You can talk about dreams with your students and how to write about them (fiction, nonfiction). Go back to how to get ideas if you need to.

Assignment:

Write about a dream for next week. Perhaps changing sleeping place (move to a different room, or the sofa) will allow dreams to happen more spontaneously.

Lesson Five

Producing Ideas through Questions

Discuss the assignment given at the end of the last lesson on writing about dreams. Select a few to read to the class, or ask for volunteers to read theirs. Have the other students comment. Encourage constructive criticism.

More Ideas

Here is a list of 15 questions that may help your students produce more ideas. Have the students write a paragraph or two for each question. Select some to read aloud, or ask for volunteers to read theirs.

1) What is your background? (Family, ethnic, religious, geographic)

2) What have you done that is unique?

3) Where have you been that's interesting?

4) Whom have you learned things from? (As a child, as an adult)

5) Whom do you know? (People around you, celebrities)

6) Have you overcome a problem that faces a large number of people?

7) From experience, do you know how to do something better, cheaper, or easier than anyone else?

8) What's wrong with your life?

9) What do you want most in life?

10) What are some of the important times of your life?

11) What interests you?

12) Have you had an adventure so unique, exciting or humorous that people will be interested in hearing about it from beginning to end?

13) How do you overcome boredom? Depression? Frustration? Sadness?

14) When did you first fall in love and why?

15) What is your favorite holiday and what does it mean to you?

***

Following is a story based on observations of a family's gatherings.

***

Christmas Chaos

The most difficult thing about cooking a large dinner is to time everything so all the dishes are ready at the same time. It's particularly difficult when there are only four burners on the stove, and your oven is only large enough to hold the turkey. And with too many people trying to lend a hand. Well, put it this way: Remember the old saying "Too many cooks spoil the broth?" Well, this can happen too.

"The element is not on," says sister as she peers in the oven. "Do you suppose it's burned out?"

"It can't be. Not today. It's Christmas."

"Calm down," says mother, as she checks the turkey and the oven. "The element does seem to be burned out, but the turkey is almost done."

"Dad! Come here!" Dad can fix everything. "The element--we think it's burned out."

Dad checks the oven. "I'm sorry, little girl, it is."

"Now what?" he answers. "We'll eat the turkey. It's done. Look." He points to the turkey. "M-m-m, smells good, too."

"Now what's that smell?" asks mother.

"Oh, no, the potatoes are sticking. When they stick, they start to burn. Dear sister here was to watch them. And stir them!"

"Me? I was making the gravy. The gravy! Oh, no! It's getting lumpy!" sister moaned.

"Idiot! You must have had the heat too high!"

"Well, it takes your precious ceramic stove forever to heat!"

"Girls! Stop it now, it's Christmas!" mother demands. "And I hear the doorbell."

It's brother and his family. Everyone exchanges greetings.

"Is your salad in a serving dish?" the hostess asks the sister-in-law.

"My salad? Oh my gosh. I forgot all about it. I'm so sorry!"

"I bet. Well, no salad for dinner, then. I have no greens, there's no store open, and there's no time to make Jello. Thanks a lot."

"Now, now, your sister-in-law meant well," consoles mother, as sister-in-law leaves the room in search for a drink.

"Sure mom, she just had the Christmas liquor on her mind."

Everyone is seated, grace is said, and mouths are watering. The dishes are brought in from the kitchen and given to father. First the turkey, then the dressing, followed by the mashed potatoes, gravy, sweet potatoes, peas, relishes, rolls, butter and jelly--and in that order, if at all possible. One year, when dishes were passed in a different order, and the gravy had been served before the potatoes, everyone put gravy on the turkey, and then after the potatoes went around, found there wasn't enough gravy for all. Some of the kids became quite upset. Such chaos!--just because of a little disruption in the order of the dishes being served.

It's funny how everyone can be so polite-- "please pass," and "thank you" at the table, when they can be so impolite away from the table. Perhaps it's because father controls the situation.

Father doesn't lecture during Christmas dinner. Everyone is polite. Father says the turkey is great. Everyone agrees. Father says the dressing is great--everyone agrees. Father finishes eating first. No one takes another helping. Everyone finishes eating. The sisters serve the dessert. Father says he wants a small piece; eldest brother asks for the same (however, he will serve himself a second piece in the kitchen later). Father says "Where's the pumpkin pie?"

"Yes, where?" everyone echoes.

"I didn't feel like making it," answers the hostess/daughter.

"It was bad enough you added peas, fresh sweet potatoes, and brown rolls--but no pumpkin pie?"

"It's my house father, and I don't like pumpkin pie! Eat your cranberry pudding!"

"Yes, madam!" retorts father.

***

This story was also rewritten later, and published, this time under the title "Why John Can't Come Home for the Holidays."

Why John Can't Come Home for the Holidays

The reason, it has been discovered, why John can't come home for the holidays is that it's too upsetting for him. The conclusion was reached by a majority of John's friends, plus his therapist.

John would relay incidents of the holidays, which helped reach this conclusion, and his diagnosis—fear of failure, and need for peace.

Like last Christmas:

"The element is not on," says sister as she peers in the oven. "Do you suppose it's burned out?"

"It can't be. Not today. It's Christmas," screamed sister, almost hyperventilating.

"Calm down," says mother.

"Dad! Come here! Quick!"

"Now what's *that* smell?" asks mother.

"Oh, no, the potatoes are sticking. When they stick, they start to burn. Dear sister here, was to watch them. And stir them!"

"Me? I was making the gravy. The gravy! Oh, no! It's getting lumpy!" sister moaned.

"Idiot! You must have had the heat too high!"

"Girls! Stop it now, it's Christmas!" mother demands. "And I hear the doorbell."

It's brother and his family. Everyone exchanges greetings.

"Is your salad in a serving dish?" the hostess asks the sister-in-law.

"My salad? Oh, my gosh, I forgot all about it. I'm so sorry!"

"I bet. Well, no salad for dinner, then. I have no greens, there's no store open, and there's no time to make Jello. Thanks a lot."

"Now, now, your sister-in-law meant well," consoles mother, as sister-in-law leaves the room in search for a drink.

"Sure mom, she just had the Christmas liquor on her mind."

"Speaking of Christmas liquor, John here appears to have a hangover. He's hardly said a word," said Dad.

"I just don't want to get in the middle of this."

"Maybe if you'd get a decent job. That job of yours is nothing. And I offered you vice presidency in my company!"

"I don't want to be a stuffed shirt behind a desk...!"

"You're calling me a stuffed shirt? Who are you to tell me...?"

"What do you expect me to do—follow you around like a little puppy?"

John gets a punch on the side of the nose. He starts to hit his father back, but his mother and his sisters stop him.

Then after Christmas, John decided it would be best if he did not return home, until he became engaged to Ann. Ann wanted to meet his parents.

Last Easter:

Nieces and nephews are decorating eggs for Easter when John arrives at his parents' home.

"Hey kids," says Grandpa, "here's John. I'll bet he can draw some pretty designs on the eggs."

"Oh, yeah?" John thought his father was referring to his good talent.

"Yeah. And at least people will admire them—not like your paintings," he added.

"Dad. Mom. Ann is here. I did bring her home as you requested. So I'd appreciate it if...."

"John does have a job now in advertising, dear," mother reminds father.

"But have you *seen* his work?"

"Hey, it sells...," defended John, as Ann walked in. "Mom, Dad, please...."

Then there was Thanksgiving:

"Dad, I've been thinking that you could use some assistance in promoting your business—like some new signs, new business cards, sales literature...."

"And I suppose you're proposing that you design it?"

"Well, I could make some valuable suggestions."

"Valuable? Valuable? You call your junk valuable?" Father was getting irate.

"Hey, I know it's not the best, but it does sell," defended John.

"Sell? Sell? Is that all you think of is selling? How about your reputation?"

"I have a good reputation. I *sell* my work!"

"That junk?" Father was getting very angry.

"Junk? You're calling my work junk? Look at the junk you sell to the consumer...."

John's plea:

John has requested that it be known to his family that if he doesn't come home for the holidays, that it has nothing to do with his love for them. He says he loves all his family dearly, but just needs peace and needs to realize he's not a failure.

***

Another story, written about a harried housewife, follows:

Can't Anyone Hear Me?

"Frank, I'm home!" yells Joann as she dashes through the kitchen door from the adjoining garage. She drops her purse and the mail on the counter, but takes some caution in placing her briefcase lid-side up, on top of a few weeks' accumulation of newspapers and junk mail. She quickly peers inside the oven.

"Damn it Frank! Why didn't you start the roast?" she demands as she quickly scans the kitchen, and spots it among a pile of dirty dishes. He never does anything I ask him to do, she thinks as she marches in a beeline toward the den. "Frank!"

"Huh?" says the half-sleeping and somewhat lifeless body on the couch. "You say something?"

"You damn right I did. Why didn't you start the roast? You know I have to be at the meeting tonight at seven."

"Meeting?" asks Frank rather sheepishly.

"Yes. The board meeting."

"I'm sorry."

I bet, says Joann to herself, as she storms off to the kitchen. I'll have to make something quick. Let's see. That rice dish. "Damn, where is that pan?" asks Joann aloud as she looks for the pan she usually cooks rice in. She spots the pan among the mountain of dirty dishes, then grabs a smaller one. "This will have to do." Why couldn't he wash the dishes, just once? she asks herself.

After having everything started on the stove, she reappears at the door of the den. "Frank, please watch the rice, it's about to boil. I have to get ready."

"M-m-m," says the lifeless body on the couch.

"I smell something burning," says Joann a few minutes later, as she rushes to the kitchen. The rice had boiled over onto the ceramic cooktop and made an ugly black and brown crusty mess.

"Frank!" she screams. "FRANK!"

The non-productive body appears. "Did you call?"

"Look what you did!"

"I did?" he asks like a squeaky mouse.

"Yes." Joann starts to cry. Frank reaches out to grab the pan, and Joann reaches out to stop him. "I'll take care of it. Please," she pleaded. Now go listen to the weather report. I want to know if I need a raincoat." That should be easy enough for him to do, she reasons.

At dinner, Joann asks Frank if the forecast said rain.

"I'm sorry, I didn't hear," he says somberly.

"Didn't hear? You were sitting right there! What is wrong with you? Don't you ever listen?" At that she gets up from the table, gathers her things, including her raincoat, and storms out the door, but not without a few last words to Frank. "Do you think you can handle a few dishes?" she asks as she gestures toward the table, and then the sink. She didn't wait for an answer, probably because she figured she wouldn't get one.

Joann was surprised to find she was the first one at the meeting, but even more surprised at 7:10, when she still was the only one there. However, by 7:20, she became furious. She called Judy (her friend, and another board member).

"Judy!" Joann panicked when she heard Judy's voice answer the phone. "Where are you?"

"What do you mean where am I? At home with Jim, of course."

"Judy, you were to reschedule the meeting for today. How could you do this to me?"

"I'm sorry, but I...."

"Don't you ever listen to me?" yelled Joann frantically, and hung up as Judy was still trying to apologize. "Some best friend."

Joann went back home, and after discovering that the dishes were not done, and that Frank had again retreated to the den, she quietly did the dishes herself, all the while complaining to herself about Frank. He is worthless—he just lays there and doesn't do a damn thing. I work to pay the bills, buy groceries, and make the house payments. Why did he have to lose his job? It's been almost a year now, and he still hasn't found work, not that he's looking too hard. The least he could do is some cooking and cleaning—and dishes. "Damn!" says Joann as she hits a glass against the sink and discovers it cracked. Why did I ever marry him in the first place? To be the provider? That's what he should be.

After she finished the dishes, she took a hot bath and crawled into bed.

It's that darn telephone again! Why do people always have to call when I don't feel like answering it? It's such an effort to get up and reach for it over there on the night stand. Well, I guess I'd better get it, or it will be important. With my luck it will probably be a wrong number. Oh well.

Joann finally reaches across the bed to the night stand, for the phone.

"Hello?"

No answer.

Joann slams down the receiver.

Joann swings her legs over the side of the bed, when she is hit with sudden dizziness. She lays back down and goes to sleep—a deep sleep. She sleeps for what seems like hours. Suddenly Joann awakes. She hears voices. It sounds like Judy.

"Judy?" Joann calls.

No answer.

"Judy?" Joann calls again.

No answer again. She is sure that was Judy's voice she heard downstairs. Who was she talking to? Why couldn't Judy hear her call out to her?

Joann hears more voices. She tries to identify them.

"I don't know. She looks dead to me," says Frank in monotone.

"Frank! Judy! Jim! I'm okay! I'm just tired!" Why don't they hear me? Joann starts to cry, but there are no tears.

Joann hears new voices. They are coming closer, entering her bedroom. Someone takes her pulse, then listens to her heart with a cold stethoscope. A doctor, she hopes. Perhaps he can tell Frank, Jim, and Judy, that she's all right. Joann tries to open her eyes, but it seems to be an impossible task. Her body feels like lead, as she can't seem to move any part of it.

"She's dead!" says the strange voice.

"No! N-O!" cries Judy.

"Oh, God!" cries Jim.

"Frank! Frank! I'm not dead! Frank tell them I'm not dead! Jim? J-u-d-y! FRANK! I'M NOT DEAD! DON'T YOU HEAR ME? I'M NOT DEAD! FRANK! DAMN YOU! LISTEN TO ME! FRANK!"

"FRANK!" Joann awakes on this last call for Frank, as she suddenly sits up in bed. Frank is sound asleep beside her. Wow, he doesn't even hear me scream, she thought.

Joann lies awake for a while, thinking about how this dream could be a basis for a great story. If she would only write it down, she could probably even get it published.

"Dream on," she said quietly as she lay back down. "But perhaps I should give it a try."

***

Another more adventurous story follows:

The Hitchhiker

"Hey, you girls want a ride?" The voice came from an old white Cadillac going in our direction.

"Sure, why not?" answered Mary, then proceeded to climb in the back seat. I followed.

Mary and I had decided to walk to town earlier that day. It was three miles, and after walking three blocks we decided to take a chance at hitchhiking. It was Mary's idea. I agreed, as it would take us a long time to walk the three miles. It only took a few minutes of walking with our thumbs stuck out at cars passing by, when one stopped.

"What you girls doing out here? Where are ya going?" asked the guy in the front passenger's seat. He was rather nice looking. Blonde hair, a bit too long though, blue eyes, sexy looking, but a little rough around the edges.

"We were just walking to town," said Mary. I let her speak as she was willing and I was rather nervous.

"What's in town?" the guy in the front passenger seat spoke again.

"Oh, we just were bored and wanted to find some fun."

Is this Mary's way of flirting? Or what? I sure wish she'd bite her tongue.

"Oh, we can show you some fun, can't we guys?" They all laughed.

"Weren't you girls afraid someone would pick you up?" asked the driver. He was older, had black hair, lacked a shave for what looked like several days, and looked quite tough.

"That's what we were hoping," answered Mary.

"But you never know who will pick you up," replied the driver.

"True. But you guys don't look too bad," said Mary.

I wish she'd shut up.

"Didn't your mother ever tell you not to hitchhike? Or not to talk to strangers?" asked the blonde guy.

"Yeah. But who listens to mothers?"

Oh, Mary, please shut up. Aren't we to town yet?

"Hey, you're pretty quiet," says the driver as he turns his head slightly, and nodded toward me.

"I'm shy," I replied.

"Haven't you ever hitchhiked before?" asked the driver.

"No," I squeaked.

"Don't worry. We won't hurt you. Animal here is shy too, aren't you, Animal? He likes you."

"Oh brother. But he is cute. And what a name—Animal.

"Hey, Brad. Talk to the girl," the driver ordered. Brad was sitting in the back seat behind the driver, I in the middle, and Mary on my right.

Brad finally spoke. "Hi, my name is Brad. What's yours?"

"I'm Sally," I replied.

"And I'm Mary."

Oh, yes, she must make sure they know who she is.

"He's Animal. He's Mike. And this is Animal's car."

"Hey, we're almost to town. Where should I drop you girls off?" asked the driver.

"The Pub is fine," said Mary.

That's a bar! Why did she say The Pub? They might decide to come in too.

"How would you girls like to go out with us sometime?" asked Mike. "And maybe you have a friend for Brad here? How about it Mary?"

It was obvious that Mike, the driver, liked Mary. And rather obvious that I was paired with Animal.

"Okay," Mary happily replied. Mike and Mary exchanged telephone numbers before we got out of the car by The Pub.

"Bye. See you later girls," they echoed.

I hope it's much later. Mary and I entered The Pub. We walked to the back of the bar to a booth, ignoring the "wolf-whistles" on the way. Perhaps it's our mini-skirts. We ordered a beer. And a while later, another.

Suddenly two guys entered The Pub. The bar became quiet, as they made their way to the back—pushing, shoving, even knocking a guy off a bar stool on the way. They sat down beside us—Mike by Mary, and Animal by me. Animal put his arm around my shoulders. I was frozen, but I imagined not as frozen as I would have been without the beers to warm me.

"Show them," said Mike to Animal.

Animal pulled out a wad of green, and ran his thumb along the side, so I could see it wasn't small bills he had. "You girls want to have some fun?"

"Sure," said Mary, her eyes were big as saucers.

"What would you like to do?" asked Mike.

"Well, I'm hungry...."

"Fine, we'll eat," interrupted Animal. "Hey, waitress!" he yelled.

"Well, that isn't exactly what I had in mind," said Mary quietly, as I think only I heard her.

Animal ordered burgers, fries, onion rings and Cokes. While we ate, he would run his hand up and down my leg. I'd push his hand away, but he'd only grab it, and twist it, until I was afraid it'd break. And I didn't dare yell.

After eating, the guys thought they'd like to go to a liquor store. We left the Pub and entered the old white Cadillac once again. They stopped at a liquor store. They were going to get some beer and whiskey. After they went in, Mary and I, who were told to wait in the car, decided that we wanted some wine. She talked me into going in, since I was Animal's date, and he had the money.

I entered just in time to see Animal flash his switchblade in front of the elderly clerk's face. Oh, how I hoped he didn't see me, but as I turned, I stumbled and knocked a bottle over. The slight crash he heard, as he yelled at me to get back in the car.

I was shook up and tears were rolling, when Animal came back. He then put his hands on my shoulders, looked fiercely into my eyes, as he sternly said: "You will do as I say. Do you hear me?"

"Yes," I squeaked.

The guys had a case of beer and whiskey and drove us outside of town near the edge of a woods where we would intoxicate ourselves and enjoy some heavy petting. After being parked in one spot for a while, we proceeded further into the woods where we spotted another car. The guys recognized whose car it was.

"It's Dan," Animal said.

"Let's go," said Mike as they both got out of the car.

The Cadillac was parked about 100 feet away from Dan's car. Mary and I heard screams while we waited but decided it was because Animal and Mike snuck up on them and frightened them, as the screams didn't last long. I don't know if we were too dumb or too scared to say anything when they came back with items of clothing from the other car—including some more intimate things. Maybe we didn't ask, as they were laughing. Or perhaps we were all too drunk.

We continued the petting. It was getting heavier than I wanted it to be, but Animal wanted more. He suddenly pulled the switchblade out of his pants pocket, opened it, and ran it up and down my stomach. He then held it to my throat and said in a very low, commanding voice, "You will do as I say. Now take it all off." As I started to remove the last items of clothing, he examined the blade of his knife.

"Keep going. Hurry it up!" I had slowed down, hoping he'd change his mind.

"Get out with your hands above your head!" It was the police.

According to the police, several teenagers in a car parked nearby had been beaten and robbed of some money and clothing items. They went to the police.

Animal and Mike were handcuffed and pushed into the police car, to be later questioned. Mary and I were later escorted home.

This was definitely an experience I could have done without—never again will I hitchhike.

***

You can discuss these stories with your students and encourage them to actively participate in the discussions.

Assignment:
1) Ask the students to take the dream that they wrote about and rewrite it to make it more interesting.
2) Write a story about a different dream than the one they wrote about before.

Lesson Six

Various Ways of Developing a Paragraph

For this class session, you can discuss with the students various ways of developing a paragraph.

NOTE: Keep in mind that you are teaching a creative writing class, so don't style this lesson like a basic English skills class.

Paragraph Development:

While it is important to develop a paragraph that contains one idea or thought, and to start another paragraph when a new idea or thought develops, many students fail to understand where the break is. To help students understand this, discuss a variety of thought patterns and the following examples.

Description:

Most good descriptive writing appeals to the reader's senses (sight, smell, taste, touch and feel). Instruct the students to use lively, specific details, and to present the descriptive details in a logical sequence.

Some possible topics are: people the students are familiar with, a big event, a favorite pastime, or a favorite food. Of course, you could always use some of the topics from earlier lessons (if you haven't used them already, after all, repetition of the same topics may serve to not only bore the students, but to stifle their creative juices).

Narrative:

To narrate means to tell a story or to give an account of. A narrative takes many forms: a novel, short story, biography, or even autobiography. Tell your students that when they write a narrative, they should try to re-create a story or experience in a way that the readers can imaginatively participate in it or relate to it.

When writing a narrative it is important to use specific details, to limit the subject, and of course, to write the narrative in some logical order.

Some possible topics to write on are personal experiences that stand out in the writer's mind as being significant, and firsts (first date, first day at college, first job).

NOTE: If you give narrative examples of your own life, be sure not to give too many personal details, so the students don't misconstrue it as a personal story.

Example:

To write an example piece means that you rely on examples for the support of the main focus, to support the main idea. Examples make the piece more concrete, clarifies, and can make the author more credible.

A writer may talk about loss of a certain object or person, and the reader may agree, but may have a different description of the emptiness he/she feels. However, by adding examples, the reader understands what the writer is feeling.

Tell your students to make sure that their examples are examples, and not generalizations, and that the thesis (or generalization) can be supported by examples. Also instruct them to be specific, and to think about the arrangement of the examples in their writing.

A possible topic is: what it means to live a healthy lifestyle.

Process:

A process is most popularly a "how-to" piece, a set of step-by-step instructions of how to make something, or do a task. It includes steps and actions that end in a desirable result if followed correctly. Therefore, it is important not to miss any steps. The explanation needs to be complete and accurate, and be in chronological order. Sometimes steps can be grouped (such as in baking a cake, the groups would be the cake and then the icing). A good writer also defines terms that could be unfamiliar to the reader, anticipates any difficulties, and tells the reader what to do if something goes wrong.

Some possible topics are: a recipe for a favorite food, how to change a tire, how to assemble something, how to be a working mother, how to give a party, how to clean the house.

Comparison and Contrast:

Comparison and Contrast shows both similarities and differences. The writer needs to be fair with comparison-contrasts, and must follow a pattern of organization (either by point or by subject).

Possible topics are: any past versus present topic (cars, relationships, attitudes), what something was thought to be like and then what it was actually like (college, relationship, marriage, vacation), two competing products (or places, eating establishments, dogs, methods of doing something), two contrasting people (by profession), two contrasting emotions (terror and fear, infatuation and love).

Classification and Division:

Classification moves from the smaller parts to the larger part, and division moves from the larger group to the smaller group.

Possible topics are: using the computer, visiting the relatives at Christmas, possible jobs, automobiles, clothing, flowers.

Cause and Effect:

Cause and effect tells why something happened. A causal chain tells of a chain of events that resulted in a cause, that in turn resulted in another cause, and so on. A cause-and-effect piece of writing should also tell why something happened.

Possible topics are: a major decision in life, romance, a major purchase, paying for school.

Definition:
Definition writing is an extended definition of something (not just a dictionary definition).
Possible topics are: happiness, freedom, wealth, hope, fun.

Argumentation:
An argumentation paper tries to persuade the reader to a particular point of view by means of logic. Sometimes argumentation is also used for a sales piece.

The writer must use logic, and while using logic, can use induction or deduction. Induction is the process of reasoning from the particular to the general, and deduction is the process of reasoning from the general to the particular.

Deductive answers why and gives an example and comes to a conclusion).

Possible topics are: reality shows are bad for the American public, the sale of tobacco should be made illegal, marijuana should be legal for medicinal purposes, dogs make better pets than cats.

Analogy:
An analogy is writing about something unrelated in order to illustrate your point.

Examples of analogies are:

Making a marriage work is a bit like cooking good food—it takes quality ingredients and devoted cooking to preparing a good dish.

Having only a few minutes to write a paragraph is like trying to buy a cart load of food at a supermarket on a Saturday afternoon!

Life is a bowl full of cherries as you never know what you'll get.

Having a fear of what people think of you is like a bull with a ring in its nose.

***

Assignments:
1) Write three paragraphs of three to five sentences on each of the nine styles above.

NOTE: If you have time for the students to write in class, have them write one paragraph type at a time, then ask for volunteers to read theirs aloud.

2) Write an analogy.

Lesson Seven

Rewriting a Story

At the beginning of this lesson, give the students the following story and have them rewrite it in class. As an option of them working on this rewrite individually, you may have them work in pairs, or in groups. Instruct them that they are to keep the main idea of the story, to rewrite it to make it better by giving the writing more lively details.

***

Philly

Yawn! Monday morning. Ah-h-h, sunrise! It is getting lighter by the minute in here. Time to get up and stretch. Soon people will be coming in to work. And soon, he will be here. Or maybe he'll stop someplace else first and get here a little later.

Good morning. My name is Phyllis. My friends call me Philly. I am a Philodendron, of a variegated breed. Such a pretty shade of green, actually, with white frosting. I guess I've become a little vain, but then, who isn't?

Oh, I remember when I used to sit in the plant section of a department store and wait for someone to pick me up and take me home with them. It's so lonely sitting in the store. Even with all the other plants. As they were all shapes and sizes, they made me feel lost in the crowd. Poor little me.

You nearly die of thirst before someone waters you. In fact, some of us do. Why, baby Fern just died the other day. Dehydration. Just about the time you think your time is up, some dumb sales clerk comes by with one of those long-spouted watering cans. First they poke you with the spout and then they nearly drown you. You have to try to swallow what you can before it runs straight through.

Then there were all the times small children (they probably don't know any better) and other idiots pick you up and play with you. And can they get rough! Once in a while one of us would get knocked on the floor and once in a while one wouldn't make it through that. In fact, my friend Violet went that way. Poor gal. And poor Alice is crippled, probably for life, ever since someone knocked her over.

Too bad we don't have insurance policies. We could collect for damage and buy a decent home. We could try to sue, but who would listen to us, anyway?

Actually, I've been pretty lucky. Being situated in the middle keeps me that way, I guess.

People don't seem to realize either, that we plants need our sleep. If we are expected to grow, we must have not only proper nutrition, but sleep. They keep those bright lights on so long sometimes. There were days I just couldn't wait until closing time, so I could take my nap.

Now don't get me wrong. We do need the light. It's just that enough is enough. I mean, it gets a little hot sometimes. In fact, one of my leaves got a little sunburned. Does that hurt!

Then came my lucky day. This nice young lady came in the store and browsed through us plants. She spotted me, and very gently picked me up. She saw my one bad leaf. "You poor thing," she said. "Take me home. Please," I pleaded. "We'll fix you up," said the lady. "Come with me." I can't believe it! Finally I'll get out of here! I'm sure I'll have a nice home.

On to the checkout counter, outside, (ah-h! So this is what fresh air is) and into her car. When she got me home, she set me by the kitchen window, alongside the kitchen sink. This, I found out later, was so I wouldn't go into shock when transplanting time came. But it was worth it, as I was transplanted into the most beautiful home, which is still mine. It is a clay pot sprayed black and has polished rock exterior all the way around. I love it!

If I thought I was going to stay in this lady's home, I was wrong. The next day she put me in a box and put me in the car. I ended up on her desk at work. I stayed there for nearly five months. That was a great spot. I would get admired for my great beauty and growth and also received many compliments on my home, especially on the rock exterior. This lady had made this pot herself. I was so proud! I had fluorescent light and got watered whenever I needed it. I even had someone to talk to me.

Then came her last day of work. She was leaving. I wondered what would happen to me. Please give me a good home. I didn't have to wonder where I was going for long, as she soon gave me to a very dear friend of hers. I am now sitting in his office. It is a little more private than before; but where I am sitting, I can see people walk by. I get water occasionally. I even get talked about on the phone. It makes me feel important. You'll never guess who talks about me. My new owner and the lady who gave me to him, of course. At least I am not forgotten. In fact, I was quite the topic of discussion among some people here as to how and why I got here.

Here he comes, with coffee in hand. He sits down, sips on his coffee, lights up a cigarette and gets right to work. I sure wish I could help, to make it easier for him. There's such a pile of papers which he'll try to make a dent in before the end of the day. There's lots of phone calls to make.

"Hi. How are you doing?"..."The plant?..."

I know who he is talking to. The lady who is responsible for my being here. The lady who rescued me from the plant section of the department store. The lady to whom I'm eternally grateful and will never forget. For her I will do everything I can to take care of her dear friend here. If only he would talk to me....

***

It may be a good idea to copy the story onto a transparency to use on the overhead projector, or have it on a computer to project to a screen. Go through the story as a class, taking the best suggestions for improvement, and rewrite and edit the story as a class.

Although the process of rewriting may be very time-consuming, it should prove to be very helpful. After this exercise, your students may even express an interest in having a similar exercise.

***

Assignment:
Rewrite the following story.

***

Both Gone

Susan's husband Tom had been out of town on business for the last four days. Tonight he would be coming home. Susan couldn't wait to see

Tom. They were newlyweds and she missed him so much when he was gone.

Tonight would be different. Susan was planning a special candlelight dinner. Dinner would be nice, yet simple. Steak, baked potatoes, tossed green salad, rolls and champagne. Tom was to be home around eight, so she planned to serve dinner soon after.

That day, Susan had gone to work, same as usual. She worked as a receptionist in an office building nearby. After work, she would stop to pick up what groceries she needed: the steaks, lettuce, green pepper, a cucumber, tomatoes, sour cream, and also the champagne and a couple nice candlesticks.

Once home, she showered, fixed her hair and put on fresh makeup. Then she went to her closet to choose something to wear. She chose a slinky, low-cut black dress, very sexy, which she bought recently but hadn't worn yet. This would be the perfect dress. She was sure Tom would like it. She laid the dress on the bed, to change into later. As first she would start dinner.

She went to the kitchen and wrapped the potatoes in aluminum foil and put them in the oven and turned it on at three hundred and fifty degrees. Then she washed the lettuce, tore the leaves and divided about one quarter of the large head into the two bowls. She then sliced some green peppers, cucumber, and a tomato and divided that among the two bowls. She put plastic wrap on each bowl and put them in the refrigerator. Then she wrapped the lettuce, green pepper, and cucumber and put them and the rest of the tomatoes in the refrigerator. Having everything put away, she cleaned up everything and set the table. She used her best dishes, placemats and cloth napkins. She put the candlesticks in two ceramic candleholders and put two champagne glasses on the table. The candles would be lighted later and the champagne was in ice. Everything finished, she went to the bedroom to dress, stopping before she left the room to turn around and admire her table.

She put the black dress on. Then she added gold earrings and her favorite cologne. After she was all dressed, she stopped and admired herself in the mirror.

Being all ready and it being a few minutes to eight, she went to the dining room and lit the candles. She would put the steaks in and salads on when Tom came home. Susan then went to the living room and sat down to watch television until Tom came home.

Eight thirty. Tom was not home yet. Nine o'clock. He had still not arrived. She was sure he'd be there soon, though. Thinking she was a little tired, she laid back on the sofa to take a nap.

Ten o'clock came and the news came on the television. Tom had been killed in a car accident on his way home, about fifty miles from where they lived.

Susan never did wake up. Before midnight, the house had burned, taking her with it. Unfortunately, by the time the neighbors had noticed the fire, it was too late.

Apparently it was started by a fallen candlestick.

***

Assignment:
Be prepared to write a book review or movie review in the next class session.

Lesson Eight

Story Rewrite

Select the best rewrites and read aloud to the class or ask for volunteers to read theirs. *Or* you may wish to do a rewrite together as a class.

Or you could share with the class the following rewrites.

Both Gone

On the surface it had seemed like any other Friday. She had gone to work at the usual time, answered her phones with her receptionist voice, greeted clients as they shook the February chill from their coats. But inside herself she felt elated—not ordinary. Tom was coming home from his four-day business trip and she wanted everything about tonight to be perfect. She had planned carefully. The dinner with the steaks they could ill afford, still paying off wedding bills, champagne, wedding china, new candlesticks, even her dress. She had laid it out on the bed this morning before work. It was seductive—yet classy. Just like Susan herself.

She didn't really like to cook. It was more fun doing things outside. Skiing, running—even just walking through snowy woods with Tom, stopping to make snow angels and laughing at the storm. Tonight she took more pride in getting the dinner right, down to the last lettuce leaf and the icing of the champagne. By eight o'clock she was finished. She admired her reflection in the mirror on the dining room walls as she lit the candles and wandered into the living room to turn on the television.

"I wonder why he's so late. It's not like him. I'll only take a short nap," she said aloud as she pulled the afghan over herself and sank into the couch.

A crowd had huddled in the street by midnight; neighbors--some of whom hadn't seen each other in months. Their faces were grey and frozen as they watched, in horror, the fireman take Susan's body from the flames and rubble. Bits of desperate conversation hung in the air.

"I never met him. I guess he traveled a lot. She was pretty, though."

"The police said he was killed in a crash fifty miles away."

"The fireman said a candlestick tipped over and started the fire."

"I wonder why she's wearing a dress like that. It's so beautiful."

And one by one they walked to their own houses, their feet crunching in the snow.

***

Bronze Candleholders

March 13. Tom had been out of town on business for the last four days. Tonight he would be coming home. Susan couldn't wait to see him, as she missed him so.

Susan was planning a special candlelight dinner. She wanted everything to be perfect. She would serve something nice and simple. She planned on serving steak, baked potatoes, tossed green salad, dinner rolls and champagne. They loved champagne. Tom was crazy about steak, and Susan needed the salad to fill her up and keep her weight down. She had already gained ten pounds since her marriage, which she attributed to the fact that Tom was a hearty eater, which for her meant she cooked a lot and ate too. Yet Tom's weight never changed. How lucky he was. He was nice and trim, and handsome too.

That day, Susan got up and went to work, the same as usual. She worked as a receptionist for a construction company. The office was nearby, so she usually walked. Today she would drive as she wanted to pick up some groceries after work for tonight's dinner.

Once at work, Susan could not concentrate, and so left early, two o'clock instead of four-thirty. She drove to the grocery store, but once there, changed her mind, and headed for Tottel's Department Store. Thinking she would buy something sexy to wear for Tom tonight, she headed for the lingerie department. She found a bright blue silky float, and a lavender gown. Heading for the dressing room, she tried the blue one first. No, that wouldn't do. It made her look too big. Then she tried the lavender one. No, that wouldn't do either. "Funny, how things always look nicer on the hangers," she thought. She got dressed and putting the two gowns back where she found them, spotted a slinky, low-cut black gown. At first she was going to forget it, but instead followed her inner instincts back to the dressing room. "It'll probably look worse on than the rest," she thought, but still put it on.

    Susan was glad there was a mirror in the dressing room. "Not bad," she said, when she spotted herself in the mirror. Discovering she had said it aloud, she covered her mouth and giggled. Then she waltzed around the small dressing room, all the while watching herself in the mirror. The gown was expensive, but she bought it anyway, being sure Tom would like it. It would be perfect.

    After having made her purchase, she now headed for the grocery store again. There she bought two rib eye steaks, lettuce, a green pepper, a cucumber, four tomatoes, and sour cream, and a couple long white candlesticks. Then she stopped at a nearby liquor store to purchase a good bottle of champagne.

    Once home, she realized it was only four o'clock, and so put the groceries in the refrigerator.

Then she showered, put on her bathrobe, brushed her hair and put on fresh makeup. She had laid the black gown on the bed, to put on after she started dinner. She was so sure Tom would like it.

She went to the kitchen and wrapped the potatoes in aluminum foil and put them in the oven to bake. After washing lettuce, she tore the leaves and divided about one quarter of the large head into two bowls. She then sliced some green peppers, cucumber, and a tomato and divided that amongst the two bowls of lettuce. She put plastic wrap on each bowl and put them into the refrigerator. Then she wrapped the lettuce, green pepper, and cucumber and put them and the rest of the tomatoes in the refrigerator.

Having everything put away, she cleaned up the counter and set the table. She would use her best dishes, placemats, and cloth napkins. She put the candlesticks in two bronze candleholders and put two champagne glasses on the table. The candles would be lighted later and the champagne was on ice. Everything finished, she went into the bedroom to dress, stopping before she left the room to turn around and admire her table.

The candleholders. They sure were pretty. Very ornate. They looked very old. How old, she didn't know. Or even if they were. Maybe they were just finished to look that way. Susan suddenly remembered the woman who gave them to her. How strange she had looked. And she mumbled something. Oh, yes, "Until March 13."

After their wedding ceremony last fall, they had gone to the reception in the church basement. While Susan was admiring the opened gifts on the gift table, she spotted the two candleholders. She had picked one up, just as someone came up behind her and said, "Pretty, aren't they?" She was so taken by surprise that she nearly dropped it. The woman caught it, and said, "They're from me. Use them in good health. Until March 13."

"Susan! Susan!" Tom had yelled from the other end of the room. "Come here!" Susan had set down the candleholder, and turned around to thank the woman and ask her what she had meant by "until March 13," but she had walked away. She then went to Tom's side. "Honey, did you see that woman who was talking to me?" she asked Tom, hoping he'd know who she was, but he said no. From then on, she never really thought about it, -- until now.

Susan shook her head, as if trying to shake those thoughts away and went to her bedroom to put the black gown on. Then she added gold earrings and her favorite cologne. After she was all dressed, she stopped and admired herself in the mirror.

Being all ready, and seeing it was a few minutes to eight, she went to the dining room to light the candles. She was expecting Tom at eight. Susan then went to the living room to sit down and watch television until Tom came home.

Eight thirty. Tom was not home yet. Nine o'clock. He still had not arrived. She was sure he'd be there soon, though. She was feeling tired, so laid back on the sofa to take a nap. Besides, if she would sleep, she'd get the woman and the bronze candleholders and how she had said, "They're from me. Use them in good health. Until March 13," out of her mind.

Ten o'clock came and the news came on the television. Tom had been killed in a car accident. A head-on collision. He had rolled over and been trapped in the car when the engine exploded. The accident happened about thirty miles from where they lived.

Susan never heard the news, as she was sleeping. Nor did she ever wake up. Before midnight, the house had burned taking her with it. Unfortunately, by the time the nearest neighbors had noticed the fire, it was too late.

Apparently, authorities said, the fire was started by a couple fallen candlesticks. in bronze candleholders.

***

The Candelabrum

March 13. Friday the thirteenth.

"Nothing had better go wrong today," thought Susan, although she didn't really consider herself superstitious. Such a beautiful day. It will be perfect," she said to herself. Yet she couldn't help but think that something might go wrong.

Why? She didn't know. Usually, when Friday fell on the thirteenth, it was just another day to her.

Another day. But today would be different, as tonight would be special. The man she loved so much had been out of town for the last four days. She had missed him so much. She hadn't wanted him to leave, but he had to, on business.

Tom was a salesman for a company that sold office supplies. Although he did work from the office, he still traveled about thirty percent of the time.

Susan had met Tom while he came to call on her boss at the construction company she worked for. She was the receptionist there. From the moment he stepped in the office, she thought he was the most handsome man she had seen in a long time. Tom, likewise, had thought her very pretty.

When he came out of her boss's office, he was grinning from ear to ear. Susan watched him as he approached her desk. He leaned over and said, "Do you want to celebrate with me?" Leaning a little closer, he said, quietly, "I just made a big sale. How about a drink?"

Susan hesitated a moment, glancing at the clock and then the work on her desk. "Now?" she asked.

"Well, I was thinking of later, but now is fine."

"Okay. It is almost quitting time." On that note she grabbed her purse and got her coat and was then off with the handsome stranger.

A stranger he did not remain for long. They went to wine and dine and then back to Susan's house, where they spent a very intimate evening.

Susan lived alone in a house near the edge of town. The house was small, but nice, about fifteen years old. There weren't many neighbors around, which made it nice on nights like these. Susan's husband, Dick, had left her months before. Why, no one seemed to know. Even Susan wasn't sure of his motives. He must have just gotten tired of her, or had found someone else, she thought. Susan got the house in the divorce settlement, but also the payments.

Susan and Tom saw each other again. And again. It got to be quite regular--about once a week.

From the first night, Susan knew Tom was married, but it didn't stop their seeing each other. Apparently, Tom's wife didn't appreciate him the way Susan did. But that was a sore subject, so was left unsaid. Yet he usually went home to his wife. Yes, usually, as a few nights he had spent with Susan, telling his wife he was out of town.

Often, Susan wondered how they could go on like this without Tom's wife knowing. Or did she?

Susan loved Tom so much, and was sure he loved her just as much. How she missed him when he'd be away. Tonight she would see him, as he planned on spending the night, having had told his wife he'd be out of town an additional night. Oh, how she couldn't wait to be in his arms again.

She was expecting him around eight.

To make tonight very special, Susan was planning a candlelight dinner. She wanted everything to be just perfect. She would serve something simple, yet nice. She wanted to serve something simple enough not to take much time away from Tom, as their time together was very precious. She would serve steak, and then she would have more time to be in his arms and for later. How nice it will be to cuddle up with a glass of champagne before dinner and more afterwards.

As Susan was still lying in bed, she was busy planning the evening. Besides steak, she would serve baked potatoes, green salad, cloverleaf rolls and champagne. They both loved the champagne. Susan figured she needed the salad to fill her up and to keep her weight down. She had already gained ten pounds in the few months she had known Tom. She attributed this to the fact that Tom was a hearty eater, which for her meant she cooked a lot and ate too. Yet, Tom's weight never changed. "How lucky he was," she thought. He was nice and trim, and handsome too.

Suddenly, realizing it was seven-fifteen, Susan jumped up. Office hours were from eight until four-thirty. After quickly preparing herself for the workday, she got in her car. Usually she walked, as the company she worked for was nearby. But today she wanted to pick up some groceries for tonight's dinner right after work.

Once at work, Susan could not concentrate, and so left early. Three o'clock instead of four-thirty.

She drove to the grocery store, but once in the parking lot, changed her mind. As long as she had extra time to kill, she would go to Tottel's Department Store to see if she could find something sexy to wear tonight.

Heading right to the lingerie department, and not knowing quite what she wanted, she spotted a bright blue silky float. Taking it off the rack, and draping it over her arm, she spotted a lavender gown, and took that one too.

Once in the dressing room, she tried the blue one first. No, that wouldn't do. It made her look too big, she thought. Then she tried the lavender one. No, that wouldn't do either. "Funny, how some things always look nicer on the hangers," she thought.

She got dressed, and then putting the two gowns back where she found them, spotted a slinky, low-cut black gown. Thinking of the two previous disasters, she was going to forget it at first, but then followed her inner instincts back into the dressing room. "It'll probably look worse on than the rest," she thought, but still put it on.

Susan was glad there was a mirror in the dressing room. "Not bad," she said, when she spotted herself in the mirror. Discovering she had said this out loud, she covered her mouth and giggled, feeling silly. Then she waltzed around the small dressing room, all the while watching herself in the mirror.

The gown was expensive, but she bought it anyway, as she was sure Tom would like it. It would make the evening perfect.

After having made her purchase, she now started for the grocery store again. There she bought two rib eye steaks, lettuce, a green pepper, a cucumber, four tomatoes, sour cream, and some long white candles. Then she stopped at a nearby liquor store to select a fine bottle of champagne.

Once home, she realized she had three hours left, as it was then five o'clock. After putting the groceries in the refrigerator, she showered and washed her hair. Then after putting on her bathrobe, she blow dried her hair and put on fresh makeup. The gown was lying on the bed, waiting to be put on after she started dinner.

She went to the kitchen, washed two potatoes, and wrapped them in aluminum foil and put them in the oven to bake at three hundred and fifty degrees. Then, washing lettuce, she tore the leaves and divided about one quarter of the large head into two salad bowls. She then sliced some green peppers, cucumber, and a tomato and divided that amongst the two bowls of lettuce. Susan put plastic wrap on each bowl and put them into the refrigerator. Then she wrapped the lettuce, green pepper, and cucumber and put them and the rest of the tomatoes in the refrigerator.

Having everything put away, she cleaned up the counter and set the table. She would use her best dishes, placemats and cloth napkins. She put the candles she had bought into the bronze candelabrum and put two champagne glasses on the table. The candles would be lighted later and the champagne was on ice. As everything was finished, for now, she went to her bedroom to dress, stopping before she left the room to turn around and admire her table.

The candelabrum. It sure was pretty. Very ornate. It looked very old. A beautiful antique. Just exactly how old, she didn't know. Susan, suddenly remembering where she got it, shuddered.

Early last fall, soon after she had met Tom, they had gone to an antique shop. Susan loved antiques, and was looking for a small table and some pictures. While she was looking over some pictures, Tom was at the other end of the shop, looking at something else. Then she spotted this beautiful bronze candelabrum nearby. She picked it up to admire it.

"Pretty, isn't it?" asked a woman's voice. The voice took her so by surprise that she nearly dropped it, heavy as it was.

"Yes, it is. How much is it?" Susan asked.

For you, honey, nothing. It's yours," said the woman. She was dressed in a black gown, and looked very strange, very distant.

"No, I couldn't just take it."

"Please. It's yours. Please take it off my hands. Please," begged the woman.

Susan thought the woman was going to cry, so said, "Okay. Thank you."

"Use it in good health," said the woman.

"Thank you," said Susan.

Susan turned to show Tom. As she walked toward him, she thought she heard the woman say, "Until March thirteenth." Just then another person in the shop started talking to the woman, so Susan didn't have a chance to ask her what she meant by that. From that day on, she hadn't thought of it again. Until now, that is.

She then shuddered and shook her head, as if trying to shake those thoughts away, then went to her bedroom to put the black gown on. Then she added gold earrings and her favorite cologne. After she was all dressed, she stopped to admire herself in the mirror.

Being all ready, and seeing it was a few minutes to eight, she went to the dining room to light the candles. Then she went to the living room to sit down and watch television until Tom came home.

Eight thirty. Tom had not arrived yet. Nine o'clock. Still no Tom. Susan was sure he'd be there soon, though. She was feeling tired, so laid back on the couch to take a nap. Besides, if she would sleep, she'd get that woman, the bronze candelabrum, and the woman's words off her mind. Why it haunted her so now, she didn't know.

Ten o'clock came and so did the news on the television. Tom had been killed in a car accident. A head-on collision. He had rolled over and had been trapped in the car when the engine exploded. The accident had happened about thirty miles from town.

Susan never heard the news, as she was sleeping. Nor did she ever wake up. Before midnight, the house had burned, taking her with. Unfortunately, by the time the nearest neighbors had noticed the fire, it was too late.

Apparently, authorities said, the fire was caused by a fallen bronze candelabrum that had been found in the living room near the body.

***

The story could be "stretched" even further, by adding more story material about Susan's interest in antiques; a discussion with the strange woman of the history of the candelabrum; more on the fire; Susan's relationship with Tom, and Susan's relationship with her ex-husband, Dick.

***

Book & Movie Reviews
For this class period have your students write a movie or book review. (They should be prepared for this class assignment, as they were told at the last class to bring an idea with them.

Here are some examples of book and movie reviews that you may want to share with your class prior to writing theirs.

Book Review on: Firestarter

Stephen King has done it again! The author who brought us such chilling novels as "Carrie" and "The Shining" scares us with another book. Charlie McGee is the indirect result of a top secret government agency testing with L.S.D.

Years earlier, a group of young college students unwittingly agree to take part in the government testing. A strange doctor oversees the experiment which takes place under the guise of a study by the college psych department.

What happens during the testing will forever change the lives of some of the participants. Two in particular will meet there and fall in love.

Andy McGee and Vicki Tomlinson discover that they each have a special talent. Andy can put thoughts in people's heads, and Vicki has the power of telekenesis. They marry and have a child not realizing what mutation may have been created by the effects of the drug used years before in the testing. The child, Charlie McGee, is a firestarter. She has what scientists call pyrokenesis: the ability to create heat just by thinking about it. As she grows, so does her power.

We follow sweet little Charlie and her father as they flee from agents working for the government who have already killed her mother, and are intent upon capturing her and using her powers for defense purposes.

When they are finally caught and sent to a secret government base, the fireworks begin as Charlie eventually tires of her captors and gets her revenge.

***

Movie Review of: Surviving

Teenage suicides have reached epidemic proportions in the United States with 50,000 attempts yearly and 5,000 teenagers succeeding. This topic was dealt with in the movie Surviving on Channel 555, Sunday night.

The movie ran a long three hours and occasionally was bogged down trying to set the stage for two teenagers reaching desperation. The boy, an under-achiever who always felt his father was perfect, was friends with a girl who was a definite over-achiever. She had never done well in school, had a few friends, and had tried to commit suicide once before. Opposites definitely attract in this movie.

As the couple gets closer, the parents begin to intervene and try to separate them. The boy's father thinks the world will end if his son does poorly in a college science entrance exam and insists on study, study, study. His son also has to be perfect like him, but the boy discovers father, the perfect Dad and husband, is having an affair, and his illusion is shattered!

    While the parents are portrayed as loving, they also find it hard to have time for their kids, and fail to see classic signs of desperation. The teenagers, sure they will never be allowed to be together, decided to commit suicide together, and eventually wind up in her garage, hot wiring the car, and falling victim to carbon monoxide poisoning.

    The real emphasis of the story was supposed to deal with the aftermath--how the families survived, support groups available, how fathers, mothers, brothers, sisters, and friends blamed themselves for causing the deaths of their loved ones, or failing to see what would happen.

    The one failure of the movie, in my opinion, was not enough emphasis on the families' survival. While it was important to set the stage for the "whys" of the deaths, I felt the movie dealt on this area too long and could have done a greater service in dealing with those who were left behind, and how they were to survive. It did, however, hold the whole family's attention and opened up a good topic for discussion.

***

Movie Review of: Terms of Endearment

Terms of Endearment is one of the rare movies that need a discussion after viewing, preferably with a close family member. Shirley McClain's character, Auroa, gets a bit out of line, pinching her baby daily in the beginning, to make certain she would live through the night. To be sure, many moms can appreciate this kind of anxiety.

The scriptwriter has named his characters well--Arona who is roaring, blustering much of the time; Emma (Debra Wingh), the sensible, Jack Nicholsen or Barrett with his head in the clouds--or the attic, whichever aspect of him you wish to observe. Flap, Emma's husband, is pictured as a bit of a "nerd" as well.

Nicholas' performance outshines the rest of the cast as an aging astronaut. In fact, much of the film deals with death and aging in a rather whimsical manner. He becomes more real by the end of the film and we see his humor with children.

A twist of events show Emma hospitalized for cancer treatment, and depicts nurses and doctors in an unfavorable light, but the manner in which she deals with her children's grieving is indeed sensitive.

This is a "must see" picture if you are a mom or a daughter or even if you *have* a mom. See it if you have moved away from home or sent a child to college. Bring a box of tissues if you are prone to crying. This is one movie that hits all emotion.

***

Movie Review of: The French Lieutenant's Woman

    A painting is only as good as its contrast in light and dark. The French Lieutenant's Woman was to me perfection in the art form of a movie. There were two distinct plots as different as blue and red. The first plot was somber, quiet, desperate and the second plot was vivacious, fun loving, and cosmopolitan.

    The first plot was a study in browns, grays, and cold blues. It was a period story of a village nestled by the sea. The opening scene showed the sea and clouds engulfing the village and sea wall. The sea and dark clouds come together in ferocious intensity producing dark bellowing puffs of salt water and rain. Amidst this morose setting the main character, The French Lieutenant's Woman was seen waiting at the sea wall for her lover. She was dressed in dark browns and rusts and projected the proper feeling to the audience of deep melancholy, emulating a slow walk and somber gaze out to sea.

    Just as my mood was adjusting to this dark, well-executed study of a deeply depressed lady in period costume, the plot stopped. There on the screen was a very sophisticated actress, dressed in modern day jeans and very affectionately studying her lines with her leading man. The sea was still out there, but it was serious, catching the light of the sun with beaches that could be used for lovers rendezvous if need be. It didn't take too long to figure The French Lieutenant's Woman (a la modern day actress) was dallying with her leading man.

So it went with the two plots intertwining. The first plot portrayed feeling of deep sadness, unrequited love and loss, but finally ended with The French Lieutenant's Woman coming out of her deep depression and being reunited with her gentleman friend. They were seen rowing in a boat with blue-green mountains in the background, and the sun giving a silhouette of perfection, solitude and happiness.

The second plot was of a modern day, happy-go-lucky, love affair between an actress and actor on location, making The French Lieutenant's Woman. They were both married and had to decide at the end of the movie to divorce their mates or return to their families. Up until the final scene, by the lake where "The French Lieutenant's Woman" and her gentleman had rowed off into the sunset, I was left guessing. As it turned out, the actress and actor returned to hearth and home. So even the endings were those of contrasts in light and dark.

***

Assignments:
1) Write a book review.
2) Write a movie review.

Lesson Nine

Making Your Writing Stand Out From the Crowd

For this class switch gears, and talk about how your students can make their writing better. Here are answers to some of the most basic and common questions.

What makes a good piece of writing?--A good piece of writing contains the following ingredients: 1) is on an interesting subject, 2) has a good title, 3) has a compelling lead, 4) contains quotes or anecdotes to support the main idea, 5) has smooth transition, 6) has colorful descriptions, 7) has a satisfying ending, and 8) is concise.

Is it important to be concise? Yes, vigorous writing is concise. Paragraphs should have no unnecessary sentences, and sentences should have no unnecessary words. Although you want to be concise, you want your writing to come to life, and the reader to feel he has actually stepped into the writing. A few colorful phrases here and there are enough to bring a piece of writing to life. Some check points to make writing more concise are

1) Check your lead.

2) Can you condense the first couple paragraphs into one or two sentences?

3) Are you using too much unimportant detail?

4) Are you over-explaining?

5) Are you sermonizing?

6) Avoid clichés.

7) Are any sentences 25 words or longer? Shorten them. (A nice sentence length is 17 words). Try to vary sentences--one long, one short.

8) Use a one-sentence paragraph here and there.

9) Use concrete details to show a character in action.

10) Eliminate the word "that" if a sentence makes sense without it.

11) Use contractions.

12) Put yourself on a word budget. Don't use 20 words if five will do.

Is a good title important? Yes. A good title should: 1) be short and crisp--six words or less, 2) tell what the writing is about, and 3) have impact or surprise.

There are different types of titles: show stoppers, questions, active voice, negative, numbers, fun titles, or "how to's," and "when's."

The basic ingredients of a good title are:

1) It has impact or surprise.

2) It states a subject that will appeal to many readers.

3) It serves as a lead or beginning that grabs the reader and wants him to read on.

4) It contains colorful words that touch the reader's senses (see, taste, smell, hear, touch).

How do you write a good lead? A good lead: 1) grabs the reader, 2) keeps him/her in his/her seat, 3) holds his/her attention, and 4) makes him/her want to read on.

Some different types of leads are:

1) The anecdote/incident lead. Using an anecdote or incident as a lead hooks the reader quickly and gets the writer into the subject of the article smoothly and gracefully.

2) The "I" or "My" lead. A personal approach which grabs the attention of many readers.

3) The introductory lead. This introduces something or someone to the reader.

4) The opening with a quote lead. This is one of the easiest leads to write.

5) The time span lead. This lead names a time. For example: ten years ago or 20 years from now.

6) The action lead. This places the reader in the middle of an incident right from the start.

How do you write a good ending? A good ending: 1) satisfies, 2) summarizes the main point of the writing, and 3) leaves the reader with something to think about. An ending is the grand finale.

Some different types of endings are:

1) **The summarizing quote ending.** Choose some quoted words that express the theme of your writing very concisely.
2) **The quote-and-finale-ending.** After using a quote, the writer then adds a few words of his/her own to give it that special touch.
3) **The anecdotal ending.** Use an anecdote that neatly summarizes your theme.
4) **The prose-poetry ending.** Used when the main purpose is to get some emotional response from the reader rather than to spur him/her into action.
5) **The echo ending.** This is a repeat of some word or phrase of significance in the writing.
6) **The straight summary ending.** A few sentences of the writer's own words.

What good does using an anecdote or quote do? It adds human interest, credibility to the point you are trying to make, and underlines or reflects the theme of the article. An anecdote or quote is a direct current that sparks life into writing, and can be used to illustrate an idea, prove a point, and also lend interest to the writing.

How do you get an anecdote or quote? Through a personal interview, a phone interview, newspapers, magazines, books, and people around you. Anecdotes and quotes add color and a refreshing change to a piece of writing.

***

Assignments:
1) Students should take a walk around their neighborhood and write each type of lead, using information from their observations.

Lesson Ten

Proper Formatting & Redundancy

You may need to instruct some your students on proper formatting of their writing. Here are some basics, which may serve as a review to other students.

Formatting

Use the following guidelines in preparing your writing:
1) Always make a backup copy for yourself.
2) Print on one side of the page only.
3) Leave one inch margins on all four sides of the page.
4) Your name and contact information go in the upper left hand corner, about one inch from the top of the page. Directly across from your name, in the upper right hand corner of the paper should be your last name and page number. If you know how to set up your computer to start numbering on the second page (as page 2), go ahead and do that. This

information should all be single-spaced.

5) If a pseudonym is used, put it in parentheses under your legal name (top left hand corner. Don't use a pseudonym unless for some particular reason you feel you have to.

6) About one-third of the way down the page in all capital letters, center the title of your manuscript. Then double space, and in small letters, center and type the word "by." Double space again and center your name, capitalizing only the first letters and initials. Here is where you put the pseudonym or pen name if you're using one. Generally, it is better to use your real name, but if you choose otherwise, your real name is still typed at the upper left hand corner of the first page.

7) Now double space twice, paragraph indent (always five spaces), and start the body of the manuscript.

8) On every page thereafter, type your last name, a dash, and the page number in the upper left hand corner. If you are using a pseudonym, again type your real name, but put the pseudonym in parenthesis behind it,

and then the page number. Single spaced below your name and page number, the title of the piece may be added, although it is not necessary. If the title is long, one or two words will do. Now double space twice, and continue your manuscript, double spacing throughout.

9) On the last page, after you've typed the last sentence, skip three double spaces and center the words "The End," or in particularly nonfiction, the old newspaper telegrapher's symbol "-30-" is acceptable.

[EXAMPLE]

[name]
[street address or PO Box]
[city, state, zip code]
[telephone number]
[word count]

                              [title]
                                by
                              [name]

        [start body of manuscript]

NOTE: I noticed that when a lot of the students were writing dialogue, that they would use the word "says" over and over (or in the past tense "said") or equally redundant words. So I came up with a list of "Over 150 Substitutes for the Word Says."

***

Over 150 Substitutes for the Words Says
The word "says" shows no emotion, lessens the dramatic effect of the speaker to the audience, and can project a sing-song, emotionless type dialogue when used repeatedly. Tell how the speaker speaks by using some of the following words instead:

accepts	confesses	finds
acknowledges	confirms	forecasts
acquaints	contends	gasps
addresses	contradicts	grunts
advances	controverts	harangues
advises	converses	illustrates
advocates	dares	imparts
affirms	debates	indicates
alleges	declaims	informs
announces	declares	insists
answers	defies	instructs
argues	delivers	jabbers
articulates	demonstrates	lectures
ascertains	denies	maintains
asserts	describes	maps

99

assumes	determines	mentions
assures	differentiates	notifies
attests	directs	observes
avers	disavows	orates
avows	disclaims	orders
babbles	discloses	outlines
balks	discourses	overlooks
breathes	discriminates	parleys
broadcasts	discusses	passes
certifies	disowns	perceives
challenges	divulges	pleads
charts	dogmatizes	pleas
chats	echoes	ponders
cites	elucidates	preaches
claims	enunciates	presents
clarifies	explores	proclaims
communicates	expresses	professes
concludes	fabricates	pronounces
concurs	feigns	propounds
confers	feuds	protests
proves	replies	stresses
publicizes	reports	suggests
questions	represents	supposes
rants	repudiates	sustains
rebuts	responds	swears
recites	retorts	teaches
recognizes	reveals	tells
recommends	reviews	terms
recounts	sermonizes	testifies
refutes	shares	theorizes
rehearses	shouts	traces

rejects	shows	utters
relates	speaks	vocalizes
releases	speculates	vouches
remarks	spouts	writes
renounces	states	yammers
repeats		

Sometimes things such as redundancy and repetition can turn the reader off. However, when trying to sell someone on some thing or idea, you *do* want to repeat it, but not continuously. Use your thesaurus to look up words that you tend to repeat too often.

You may also want to talk about other words that are redundant. If you have time, you can, as a class, make lists for substitutes of those words.

***

Assignment:
1) Make a list of words that you think are redundant.

Lesson Eleven

Avoiding Common Errors

For this class you could talk about common errors and how they are misused and how they can be corrected.

Some common errors are:
- the use of commas
- using the word "whether" instead of "weather" and vice versa
- the difference between "it's" and "its"
- when to use "their," "there," and "they're"
- capitalization of proper names
- when to spell out numbers and when to use numerals
- the use of the semi colon
- why paragraphs should be indented
- the use of run-on sentences and incomplete sentence fragments
- the use of single quotes
- the importance of consistency in style
- the shifting of tenses
- the use of "then" and "than"
- the use of "a long" and "along"
- short stories in quotation marks

- names of books in italics
- other misused words: stare/stair; wife's/wives; here/hear; though but/though/although; toward/towards; been/being; through out/throughout; lifes/lives; your/you're; over all/overall

***

Here is a list of words that I usually give to my students as a spelling test. These words were chosen as they were seen as some of the most commonly misused words that I had noticed in their writing. You may find additional words.

daughter
ambitious
enjoyment
chronological
mashing
confusing
organize
classify
categorize
realized
exaggerating
grateful
although
all right
appetizers
analyze

criticize
embarrass
familiar
license
schedule
hotel
liar
inconspicuous
families
awful
judgment
liable
phenomena
parameters
unique
ultimate

argument   whether
believe   implement
conscience   immigrate
convenient   contagious

***

Assignment:
1) Make a list of commonly misspelled words.

Lesson Twelve

Using Starter Sentences

For this lesson have your students write one page or more on several of the following starter sentences.

As I've always been afraid of the dark....
If money only grew on trees....
This Christmas will be the best Christmas ever....
Sometimes my words fall on deaf ears....
Now that Sue has married Dan....
On Thanksgiving Day, I plan to....
What I like most about writing is....
The first time I fell in love, it felt like....
I can't wait until summer, because then I can....
This will be the greatest Halloween ever because....
While watching the World Series....
I am looking forward to the New Year, as it will bring....
I like Valentine's Day because....
As my sock pile slowly diminishes....
While driving in my car, I sometimes....
My ideal mate would have....
The sight of motorcycles cruising down the freeway....

This summer is the greatest because....
I like to imagine myself being....
The craziest thing happened to me this summer....
This Christmas will be different because....
My idea of a Minnesota winter is....
My next door neighbor looks like....
My vacation plans for this summer are/were better than ever because....
The sand blew in my face as I....
As I rode the elevator to the office....
As the deer appeared in front of....
She screamed as I....
The others didn't stop running, but....
Though I struggled to finish, I could hear....

***

Assignments:
1) Make a list of other starter sentences.
2) Write a four to five page story using one of the above starter sentences.

Lesson Thirteen

Good Writing

For this class you could again discuss how to write a good piece of writing, and go into more detail.

Creating a Good Piece of Writing

Many aspiring writers have talents that outweigh their success in having their writing read, because they can't seem to mold their writing into a piece that is interesting and good.

How does one write a good piece? First of all, it must contain the following seven components:

1) an interesting subject
2) a good title
3) a great lead
4) smooth transition
5) colorful descriptions
6) tight writing
7) a satisfying ending.

An Interesting Subject

Explore your life for topic material. Your trade or hobby, or personal experiences, are all good sources for interesting subjects. Perhaps you collect something unusual or have had a unique experience. Don't think that your life is too boring to write about--imagination and creativity can breathe life into any topic.

I'm sure we all know at least one person who seems to have unique and exciting experiences quite frequently. Like the person who always says, "Guess what happened now!" or "You'll never believe this one!" That person and his/her experience(s) would probably be good material to write about. If you are afraid to write about someone else for fear he/she wouldn't like it, fictionalize it--change the names, the characters, places, and other sure give-away.

If you still can't think of any topic unique enough to write about, read through a newspaper, or magazine, and try a different approach to a topic or situation. This can make an old topic interesting, and can spark the editor's interest, which is what a writer needs to do to make his/her writing more saleable.

A Good Title

A good title is necessary in attracting the reader's attention. A good title should be short and to the point--six words or less. The title of your writing should spark interest in the reader.

NOTE: The title of a book however, can be changed by the editor because the title sells the book. If you're looking for books of a particular author, it doesn't matter what the title is, because you see that there is a new book out by this author and you buy it. But as a new author, you need to have a really eye-catching title (and an attractive cover on the book) because that is what makes people pick it up and buy it. And then of course, the writing, the lead etc. are important.

When a reader purchases a certain magazine, however, he/she does so because he/she already knows what type of articles or reading the magazine contains. The reader goes to a bookstore to buy a magazine, because he/she desires this particular magazine, or purchases it while waiting in line at the grocery store, because the title and contents interest him/her. The reader, therefore, is sold on the title of the magazine. Now when the reader flips through a magazine, he/she reads the titles of the various articles. If that interests him/her, then he/she reads the first sentence or the first paragraph, and if it still holds his/her interest, he/she keeps on reading to the end. Therefore, if you're writing and hoping to get it published in a magazine, your writing really needs a good title.

The title should tell what the article is about, and have impact or surprise.

There are many types of titles. Some examples are:

- Show stoppers ("Avoid Costly Rip Offs")
- Questions ("Where is Ralph?")
- Active voice ("Let Me Out of This Prison")
- Negative ("No Wheelchair For Me")
- Numbers ("60% of Victims are Transients")
- Fun ("Ding! Dong! The Witch is Dead!")
- How-to's ("How to Start Your Business on a Shoe String")

- When's ("If I Should Die Before I Wake")

The basic ingredients of a good title are that it:

1) has impact and surprise
2) has an appealing subject to many readers
3) serves as a lead or beginning that grabs the reader's attention
4) has colorful words to hook the reader's senses (the senses being: see, taste, smell, hear, touch), or portrays an image.

In writing fiction, one can use titles in the form of:

- Questions (example: "Can't Anyone Hear Me?")
- Mystery (example: "The Secret Behind the Red Door")
- Shockers (example: "My Husband Told Me He's a Werewolf")

Titles often appeal to our needs--psychological, physical, and emotional, and are the first thing the reader sees (excluding the physical appearance of the writing), so as a writer you should put some thought into your title.

A Great Lead

A great lead attracts the reader's attention, keeps his/her attention, and makes him/her want to read on.

Some different types of leads are:

1) **The Anecdote/Incident Lead.** Using an anecdote or incident as a lead hooks the reader quickly and gets the reader into the subject of the writing smoothly and gracefully.

EXAMPLE: "Making a marriage work is a bit like cooking good food--it takes quality ingredients and devoted cooking to preparing a good dish."

2) **The "I" or "My" Lead.** A personal approach that grabs the attention of many readers.

EXAMPLE: "My son weighed only twenty-six pounds at four years of age. His behavior was erratic, but doctors could not find much wrong."

3) **The Introductory Lead.** This introduces something or someone to the reader.

EXAMPLE: "You have just had a baby and still have that potbelly. You can't seem to fit back into those favorite jeans you wore when you were four months pregnant. To top it all off, someone just asked when you are due. If this is you, the following exercises will help to flatten your stomach and trim your waistline."

4) **The Opening with a Quote Lead.** This is one of the easiest leads to write.

EXAMPLE: "If you like your stories murderous and complex, with love, adultery and suspense, then 'Where is Ralph?' is waiting for you, says....

5) **The Time Span Lead.** This lead names a time.

EXAMPLE: "'In four years you will be confined to a wheelchair,' said my doctors eight years ago."

6) **The Action Lead**. This places the reader in the middle of an incident right from the beginning, and can be done with dialogue.

NOTE: If you can't think of a lead, start writing in the middle, and then go on, but keep writing. Sooner or later, and with some careful thought, you'll think of that great lead.

Smooth Transition

Smooth transition is important because it keeps the reader's interest, and keeps him/her from getting lost in the writing. You should think of transition as the glue that holds the parts together. A good way to know if you have achieved smooth transition is to get reactions from other writers and readers. They are not as familiar with the topic as you are, and may be objective enough to give you constructive criticism. If they question inconsistencies of facts or logic, it may be due to kinks in transition, as every train of thought should make logical sense to the reader.

When you are checking someone else's work for smooth transition, read through the manuscript rapidly, then if you find you have to go back to something previously read, because you think you missed something, then there is a problem with the transition, as if something is lost.

Colorful Descriptions

Colorful descriptions are important because they make the writing come alive, put the reader in the right place and time, and can project an image. Colorful descriptions can be projected through

1) action
2) dialogue
3) thoughts
4) reactions of the main or supporting characters
5) statements from the author or narrator
6) by using mechanical devices (such as a cellphone or answering device)

NOTE: Using a cellphone is a good way to add colorful description to a piece of writing. This is a good way to add a colorful description, because you get an idea of what the person is like who is answering the phone, and also the person who is on the other end of the phone, whom you don't really see. (When you are writing, you have to visualize this.) You can portray two different characters, even though only one character is talking, as you get the supposed reactions of the other person from what is said to him/her.

Another mechanical device is the answering device. You get an idea of what a character is like, and his attitudes, by what messages are left on the answering device and his/her reactions to the messages.

Both these mechanical devices--the telephone and the answering device--can portray a very colorful description of character(s).

Another way to add color to an article and a refreshing change to a piece of writing is by using an anecdote or quote. An anecdote or quote increases human interest and credibility to the point you are trying to make, and underlines or reflects the theme of the writing--it is a direct current that "sparks life" into writing. It can be used to illustrate an idea, prove a point, and also lend interest.

How do you get an anecdote or quote? Through a personal interview, a phone interview, newspapers, magazines, books, and from people around you. You can also get a book on quotes in a library or a bookstore.

Tight Writing

It is important to be concise. Paragraphs should have no unnecessary sentences, and sentences should have no unnecessary words. Some check points to make writing more concise are:

1) Do you have a good lead?
2) Could the first couple paragraphs be condensed? Many times when you have written a piece, you may find that if you take off the first paragraph or two, you may have a good piece. Some writers make the mistake of having too much description in the beginning. (Some

writers also have this problem with the ending.)

3) Could you eliminate the first and/or last paragraph?
4) Is there too much unnecessary detail?
5) Are you using unnecessary adjectives? You don't need a whole string of adjectives to describe something, instead select one or two good ones.
6) Are you over-explaining?
7) Does it sound like you are giving a sermon? This is particularly important when writing for juveniles.
8) Are you using unnecessary clichés?
9) Have you shown your characters in action?
10) Have you eliminated the word "that" when the sentence makes sense without it? Also the words "very" and "so."
11) Have you used contractions when possible? A time when you don't want to use a contraction (other than in legal writing), is when you are presenting an argument and when you want to add emphasis.
12) Have you eliminated other unnecessary words?

A Satisfying Ending

A good ending, in order to be satisfying, summarizes the main point of the article, and leaves the reader with something to think about. An ending is the grand finale of your article.

Some types of endings are:

1) **The Summarizing Quote Ending.** Choose some quoted words that express the theme of your writing very concisely.

2) **The Quote and Summary Ending.** After using a quote, the writer then adds a few words of his/her own to give it that special touch.

3) **The Anecdotal Ending.** Use an anecdote that neatly summarizes your theme.

4) **The Prose/Poetry Ending..** Try this ending when the main purpose is to get some emotional response from the reader rather than to spur him/her into action.

5) **The Echo Ending.** This is a repeat of some word or phrase already in the writing.

6) **The Straight Summary Ending.** This ending is a few sentences of the writer's own words.

If your writing contains these necessary components, it should be a good piece.

Assignments:
1) Taking a favorite piece of your writing from this course, analyze it to see if it has the above components.
2) Using the writing in Assignment #1, rewrite it using the above components.

Lesson Fourteen

Creative Writing Exercises

For this lesson you could concentrate on more creative writing exercises. One of the most popular is the Character Sketch. First ask your students to take a piece of paper and number from one through 20. Then read the questions and have them write their responses. Tell them that they can make them up as they go.

Character Sketch

The Character Sketch exercise is a great way to focus on a character (real or fictional, or a combination of both).

1) What is the sex of your character?
2) What is the age of your character?
3) How tall is your character?
4) Is your character skinny, trim, or heavy?
5) What is the character wearing? What is the style of his/her clothes? Are they clean? Or dirty? Torn? Patched?
6) Look at the character's shoes. What kind are they? Tennis shoes?

Boots? Heels? Are they new? Well worn? Polished?

7) Look at the character's hands? Are they baby soft? Work worn? Dirty? Well-manicured?

8) Is the character wearing a ring? What kind of ring is it?

9) Is the character wearing a watch? On which wrist?

10) Is the character wearing other jewelry? A bracelet? A neckchain? Beads? Earrings?

11) What is the character's hairstyle like?

12) What is the character's hair color?

13) What color eyes does the character have?

14) What is the expression in the character's eyes? Is it sad? Is it happy? Do you see pain?

15) Look at the character's nose. Is it big? Small? Crooked?

16) And the character's ears. Are they big? Small? Do they stick out?

17) Now look at the character's mouth. Is there a smile? A frown? Can you see the character's teeth? Is there anything about his/her teeth that is noticeable?

18) What is the character's favorite saying?

19) What is the character's favorite thing to do?
20) What is this person doing now?

Assignments:
1) Now write a dialogue between yourself and this character. Write one to two pages.
2) Then try adding a third person to the dialogue, and write two-three more pages.
3) Using the Character Sketch, make up another character by answering the questions differently. Now write another one to two pages.

Lesson Fifteen

More Writing Exercises

For this lesson, you can present these creative exercises. Let's start with "Settings."

Settings

Setting exercises are a great way to zoom in on a particular place. Try this one:

Imagine being in a kitchen as a small child. It could be your mother's kitchen, an aunt's, a neighbor's, or a friend of the family's kitchen. Look around the kitchen. What do you see? Where is the sink? What type of sink is it? A double sink? A single sink? What is in the sink--anything? Dirty dishes perhaps? Or is the sink spotlessly clean? Now look at the stove. What kind of stove is it? Is there something on the stove? In the oven? What? Now notice the refrigerator. Is it new? Or old? Open it. What is inside? Your favorite snack or beverage perhaps? Now notice the cabinets. Are they new, newly refinished, or marred? Is there anything unusual about them? Is there a window in the kitchen? Is there a table in the kitchen? Is it used for eating? Who is in the kitchen? What is he/she doing? What are you doing? Do you notice any smells? What are they? What time of day is it?

Now write one to two pages describing this kitchen.

Select a few stories to share with the whole class, or ask for volunteers to read theirs aloud.

Now place a character into the setting.

Again, select a few to share with the whole class, or ask for volunteers to read theirs aloud.

This type of exercise can be done for each room or setting that you use, or plan to use, in a piece of writing.

Dialogue

This exercise is great for writing dialogue.

Dick and Sally go shopping. They are going to buy one of these items: a washing machine, a new vehicle, or a TV. Write a page or two of their conversation regarding shopping for one of these items.

Ask for volunteers to read theirs aloud to the class.

Questions

Read these questions to your students, and have them write their responses.

1) Who named you? Does that name have a particular meaning? What is the potential of the name?
2) Did you have a nickname as a child? Why? Who gave you the nickname?
3) What is your favorite fairy tale? What is your favorite character in that tale? How do you relate to that

character? How do other people think you relate to that character?

4) What is your favorite song, book, or play? Why?

5) Do you remember as a child ever deciding to never again feel a certain feeling?

6) What did life promise to be at age five? At age 13? At age 18? At age 21? At age 30? At age 40?

7) What is the best thing you can do with your life? What is the worst thing?

8) What do you want to do with your life?

9) Are you a winner or a loser? When did you decide?

10) Who was or is your favorite person or idle?

11) What do's and don'ts did your mother live by?

12) What did your father tell you to do?

13) What do you believe your parents expect of your life?

14) Do you have a reoccurring dream? What is it?

15) What is your favorite motto?

16) Imagine being in a beautiful garden. What are you growing?

17) What is the most important thing you have to do right now in your life?

18) What do you see yourself doing in the future?
19) What do you do for recreation? Do you enjoy it?
20) Do you enjoy spending times with all your friends? Why or why not?
21) How did your parents deal with problems?

Now have your students select one of these questions and write one to two pages. Have them share it with the class by reading aloud.

Assignments:
1) Select a room in your home. Describe the room.
2) Listen to dialogue around you at the mall, at an event, or in school. Write a story using that dialogue.
3) Select a question from above and write one to two pages.

Lesson Sixteen

Current Events

I like to choose current events to have my students write about. Some of the ones I have chosen in the past, which can still be used today are:
1) concealed weapon laws
2) road construction
3) road rage
4) the cost of allergy drugs, and their effectiveness
5) the rising cost of health insurance and its cause
6) how one's credit report can be marred and/or fixed
7) child neglect
8) new diseases
9) popular diets
10) life as an American

Select one of these to have your students write about in class. When they are finished, have a few volunteers share theirs with the class by reading aloud. Invite the other students to comment on what they hear, and to give constructive criticism.

This is a good time to introduce the Feedback for Classmates form that follows. Have the students answer the questions for each of the readers.

Feedback for Classmates

Writer's name: _____ Your name _____

Topic: _____

1. What were the strengths and weaknesses of the writing?

2. Who is the audience?

3. Does the topic/subject and the way the piece is written meet the required assignment?

4. Is the writing organized logically? If not, how could it be improved?

5. Was the introduction clear? If not, how could it be improved?

6. Did the conclusion provide summary and/or recommendation? If not, how could it be improved?

7. Overall, what did you like best about the writing?

Stories About Us

The following starter sentences can engage the writer in personal references toward going forward in life: Read the questions, and have the students jot down their answers.

1) When I think about being of legal age, I think of....
2) When I think about middle age, I think of....
3) As I become older, I want to make sure I am....
4) I fear aging because....
5) Aging can be a positive experience because....
6) Some of the best times of my life have been....
7) Some major obstacles in my life have been....
8) Going forward in life I want to....
9) I describe myself to others as....
10) Others describe me to others as....

Now have the students select one of the above questions and write one to two pages. Again, share by reading aloud, and use the Feedback For Classmates form.

Sayings

Have the students write explanations of these famous clichés:
1) flying by the seat of my pants
2) raining cats and dogs
3) don't put the cart before the donkey
4) it's all downhill from here
5) don't put all your eggs in one basket
6) shooting from the hip

Have your students write responses to the Sayings in one to two paragraphs.

Famous Sayings

Use famous sayings from famous people. A few favorites are:

Obstacles are those frightful things you see when you take your eyes off the goal.
                                        Henry Ford

The world is a great book; he who never stirs from home, reads only a page.
                                        Saint Augustine

Have the students write a page beginning with the above Famous Sayings.

Assignments:
1) Write a story that is a comedy of errors.
2) Write a story about something that got out of control.

Songs

Using lyrics from popular songs is a good device to get the creative juices flowing. Read the lyrics and have the students write their responses.

Employee-Related Situations

You more than likely may have students who are looking for jobs. So they may appreciate these scenarios to write about to help them creatively prepare for the job hunting process or for performance on the job they may secure.

1) You need to tell an employee that they have been doing a procedure wrong for some time now, and it has been causing problems, including having a negative effect on the employee's performance.
2) You are to give a performance review, and it is not all positive.
3) You need to ask an employee to be more punctual.
4) You need to ask your boss for shorter working hours.
5) You're going to ask for a raise, but don't want to jeopardize your job.
6) You're bored with your job that you started several weeks ago, and you want to ask for more responsibilities.
7) You're overworked and you want to lessen your responsibilities.
8) Your boss wants you to work during a time you have planned a vacation out-of-town.
9) You need extra time to complete a project.

10) You are to ask your boss to support your request to attend a convention in Las Vegas.
11) You need to confront an employee whom you found out does not have his/her GED.
12) You have been offered a new position, and now you need to negotiate a salary.

These employment based scenarios might also be appreciated.

Cost Analysis. On a major freeway, there is 10 miles of road construction. Would it be more cost effective to do road construction one mile at a time? Would it result in less traffic congestion? Prepare a speech persuading authorities that it would be more cost effective.

Marketing. Prepare a speech persuading a marketing firm to take on your exercise video. Your video is different: you don't need equipment, don't need to wear shoes, and is a great fat burner that can be used by people of all shapes, sizes, and ages.

Employee Meeting. Your boss has requested that you organize a company picnic and that you do it in a way that all employees will want to attend--and to keep it in good taste. In the past, the company picnics have been boring to most, even to yourself. Prepare a speech to give to fellow employees at a company meeting to persuade them to come. Include your program of events, etc.

365 Writing Ideas

Here are some more great ideas to write on for every day of the year.

January 1
the traditional New Year's fare and whether or not it is still served today

January 2
the obsession with the bowl games and why

January 3
the history of the First babies in your city

January 4
how inmates spent the holidays

January 5
how the poor spent their holidays

January 6
Do we have the four freedoms (freedom of speech, freedom of worship, freedom from want, freedom from fear) that Franklin D. Roosevelt expressed in his message to Congress in 1941

January 7
the First Presidential Election in the U.S. and how it differs from today

January 8
future plans of big businesses

January 9
how small businesses survived the holidays

January 10
Sinclair Lewis who died in 1951, and what he would say about Sauk Centre, Minnesota today

January 11
the winter weather and how it compares to other winters

January 12
sports forecasts and record breakers for the year

January 13
new educational programs

January 14
winter activities in your area

January 15
Martin Luther King's birthday and how he contributed to society

January 16
inside activities for small children

January 17
drunk driving laws and their effectiveness.

January 18
law enforcement in your community as compared to other neighboring communities

January 19
policewomen and their burnout on the force

January 20
women in male-dominated careers

January 21
males in female-dominated careers

January 22
jobs of the future

January 23
telephones today compared to years ago
January 24
why people really use woodstoves
January 25
ways to conserve energy
January 26
high energy foods
January 27
Vietnam Day, and what it means today
January 28
the history of popular diets
January 29
a rare gift shop and its owner
January 30
a rare book dealer and rare books
January 31
the most popular books today compared to years ago
February 1
the most popular bed and breakfasts in your area
February 2
Ground Hog Day, and whether local citizens believe in the ground hog
February 3
safe driving in snow storms
February 4
a prominent business person
February 5
the secretary behind a successful business person

February 6
the wife or woman behind a successful business person
February 7
unique self-employment opportunities
February 8
accidents in sports, and sports injury clinics
February 9
insurance fraud
February 10
health insurance "deals"--are they really so great?
February 11
National Inventors Day and how it's observed
February 12
Abraham Lincoln's birthday and what he would think of our government today
February 13
a local pawn shop and items most pawned
February 14
Valentine's Day and how many things come heart-shaped
February 15
whether or not junk mail is really junk
February 16
a local distributor of magazines and books
February 17
how produce is kept fresh during transportation
February 18
dancing as exercise

February 19
a well-known chef in the community
February 20
John Glenn Day, and the first orbit of earth by U.S. astronaut
February 21
why a furnace should be cleaned, and how it was cleaned years ago as compared to today
February 22
George Washington's birthday, and what he would think of our government today
February 23
the most popular spots for singles to gather
February 24
a local publisher and the publishing business
February 25
sports activities in a local prison
February 26
state car auctions, and how the cars that are auctioned are obtained
February 27
a local astrologist and some predictions
February 28
a psychologist engaged in dream study
March 1
a local dairy farmer and the dairy farming business
March 2
a local psychic and his/her clients
March 3
the history of a local courthouse or city hall

March 4
how snow used to be a blessing, and is now a nuisance
March 5
why our highways are salted when it harms our automobiles
March 6
activities for senior citizens
March 7
the words misspelled the most often
March 8
youngsters in business
March 9
a local patent attorney and his work with inventors
March 10
a local writers' club
March 11
the history of an acting theater
March 12
stamp collecting as a hobby and the trends over the years
March 13
the university press in your state and what is published
March 14
the workings of a historical society
March 15
the Battle of the Carolina's and whether or not President Andrew Jackson was born in North Carolina or South Carolina in 1767

March 16
Black Press Day and how the Black presses affect the world of publishing
March 17
St. Patrick's Day and how it is observed today
March 18
the latest dental equipment and processes
March 19
what is involved in being a private investigator
March 20
the anticipation of spring
March 21
Earth Day and what it means
March 22
a famous person from your state
March 23
Liberty Day and famous declarations made on this day
March 24
silk flowers versus real flowers
March 25
a dietitian at a city jail and any special foods needed
March 26
a local artist and his/her work
March 27
a local seamstress and whether or not there are more females who need alterations than males
March 28
ways to save money

March 29
roller skating and popular places to roller skate
March 30
homemade aircraft and the owners
March 31
the baggageman at the airport, how many times luggage gets lost, and how much luggage is checked in
April 1
Fools Day, and the greatest jokes
April 2
wholesale clubs and their affect on the community
April 3
the Pony Express born in 1860
April 4
a sewing machine repairman and antique sewing machines
April 5
Pocahontas marriage to John Rolfe in 1614
April 6
whether or not Robert Peary was really the first man to reach the North Pole (1909)
April 7
the variety of mail-order catalogs
April 8
Good Will operations
April 9
tips from a local professional photographer
April 10
fruit trees grown in the area.

April 11
physically handicapped people and their accomplishments
April 12
ideas for gardening
April 13
major airline service in your city and ways to improve service
April 14
President Abraham Lincoln's assassination by actor John Wilkes Booth
April 15
how the Titantic sunk
April 16
unusual signs and billboards
April 17
truck drivers that come through your city, and local truck stops
April 18
dial-a-date dating services and how they really work
April 19
crisis phone hotlines
April 20
Adolph Hitler's birthday, and how society feels about him today
April 21
guided tours in your community
April 22
Arbor Day and the history of planting trees and shrubs on this day

April 23
the motion picture shown for the first time in New York City in 1896
April 24
how to use the local library
April 25
the history of waterwheels and how waterwheels are used today
April 26
bus transportation
April 27
salaries of top public officials
April 28
the Mutiny on the ship Bounty
April 29
the inner workings of the crime lab at your police department
April 30
the first television broadcast from the Empire State Building in 1939
May 1
May Day, the Maypole, and May baskets
May 2
the survival of the fiddler
May 3
local nursing homes
May 4
how four students lost their lives in anti-war demonstrations at Kent State University in Ohio in 1970

May 5
how Christopher Columbus discovered Jamaica
May 6
a male hair stylist and his clients
May 7
campus police and problems encountered on campus
May 8
local modeling careers
May 9
how Mother's Day was first observed in 1914
May 10
Golden Spike Day. Where is the golden spike that linked the railroads of the East and West?
May 11
race care driving
May 12
how National Hospital Day has been observed since 1921
May 13
the history of men's hats
May 14
the marriage laws in your state versus other states
May 15
how the first regular airmail service was inaugurated in the United States in 1918
May 16
the latest food craze
May 17
kite flying, various kites, and kite stores

May 18
how the Selective Service Act was adopted in 1917
May 19
the increased/decreased popularity of marble shooting
May 20
the adventure of Amelia Earhart who started the first solo flight across the Atlantic Ocean by a woman in 1932
May 21
what the Democrat National Convention was like when first held in 1832
May 22
Maritime Day. This was the beginning of the voyage of the first transatlantic steamship (Savannah) from Savannah, Georgia in 1819. How does this affect us today?
May 23
graduation preparations in your area, and suggestions
May 24
mobile libraries
May 25
how armored cars are built and special devices they have
May 26
the most unusual organized sport in the community
May 27
a local country club--the management, the history

May 28

the affect U.S. copyright law has had on us since it was passed in 1790

May 29

unlocking locked cars

May 30

a newspaper clipping service and how it works

May 31

training horses for racing

June 1

Statehood Day, honoring Kentucky and Tennessee

June 2

the first president to be married in the White House in 1886--Grover Cleveland, and the marriage ceremony

June 3

bird watching

June 4

the ten most popular wedding gifts

June 5

how World Environment Day was first observed by members of the United Nations

June 6

whether there is such a thing as love at first sight

June 7

a popular local columnist

June 8

a local alcoholism treatment program

June 9

avid readers of horoscopes

June 10
airplanes that are for rent
June 11
Kamehameha Day, and how King Kamehameha won control of Hawaii in 1792
June 12
the birthday of Anne Frank, and how her hiding from the Nazis is similar to those who hide from terrorists today
June 13
the technology of newspapers and comparisons of presses used today to those of yesterday
June 14
Hawaii formed as a territory in 1900, and celebrations that occur today
June 15
where we would be now if Charles Goodyear had not received a patent for rubber vulcanization in 1844
June 16
summer fashion trends
June 17
road construction hazards
June 18
rock collecting
June 19
how Father's Day was first observed in 1910
June 20
the anticipation of summer and summer activities

June 21
where farmers would be today is Cyrus McCormick had not invented the reaper in 1834
June 22
summer activities for children of working mothers
June 23
puppetry and puppet shows
June 24
the dying railroad--or is it?
June 25
singing telegrams
June 26
taxidermy
June 27
Helen Keller (born 1880) and her effect on the sight and hearing impaired today
June 28
a local shoe repair shop
June 29
house painting and do-it-yourself tips
June 30
how the U.S. Fish and Wildlife Service was created in 1940
July 1
the most popular consumer complaints in large department stores
July 2
procedure manuals, and their popularity in businesses

July 3
a profile of an investment counselor or financial advisor
July 4
how Independence Day was first observed in 1776
July 5
making a creative home video
July 6
the art of auctioneering
July 7
the most popular local golf resorts
July 8
canning tips and recipes
July 9
the Meals on Wheels program for the elderly
July 10
home nursing services
July 11
tatting-is it a lost art?
July 12
the most popular summer snacks
July 13
a local popular writer
July 14
tattoos
July 15
the local zookeeper, a day at the zoo
July 16
the first atomic bomb that was set off near Alamogordo, New Mexico in 1945

July 17
where we would be if the U.S. hadn't received Florida form the Spaniards in 1821
July 18
hospital admission and information deemed necessary before admittance
July 19
drowning victims, and safety water precautions
July 20
the country's awe when Neil Alden Armstrong became the first moon walker in 1969 **July 21**
what Ernest Hemingway would think of literature today
July 22
local chemical waste and pollution
July 23
Indian relics found in the state
July 24
water tubing
July 25
forest fires
July 26
what George Bernard Shaw would think of social problems today
July 27
what would have happened if the Korean Was had not concluded in 1954
July 28
check fraud

July 29
a woman barber
July 30
excuses used to get out of work
July 31
bicycle racing
August 1
how the United States completed its first census in 1790
August 2
how Jack McCall killed "Wild Bill" Hickok in Deadwood, South Dakota in 1876
August 3
Christopher Columbus's departure from Palos, Spain in 1492
August 4
the "hottest" picnic spots, and traditional picnic fare
August 5
walking tours in the area
August 6
wax museums in your state
August 7
the county fair
August 8
quilt making, and popular patterns
August 9
new educational programs at local schools for handicapped children

August 10
what the Smithsonian Institution was like when it was first established in 1846 as compared to today
August 11
the life of a disc jockey
August 12
whether or not we would have compact discs if Thomas A. Edison had not invented the phonograph in 1877
August 13
photographing wildlife
August 14
why Social Security was approved in 1935
August 15
how Napolean's Day has been observed since 1769
August 16
the colors of the rainbow and how it is used in art and literature
August 17
windmills as a source of energy, and as a decor
August 18
what happened to the family of Virginia Dare, the first English child born in 1587
August 19
National Aviation Day, and Orville and Wilbur Wright
August 20
renting movies from the local library
August 21
the history of the wishing well

August 22
how profitable parking ramps are
August 23
local gift and clothing consignment shops
August 24
the day the White House burned, 1814
August 25
a local wrestler and his other sporting interests
August 26
the 19th amendment which has granted women the right to vote since 1920
August 27
photographing animals
August 28
part-time farming
August 29
the most unusual business cards
August 30
raising birds
August 31
a local cartoonist
September 1
back-to-school fashions
September 2
the history of photocopying machines
September 3
coin collecting
September 4
how Los Angeles was founded by Felipe de Neva in 1781

September 5
juvenile shelters
September 6
how President William McKinley's wife went into shock after he was shot years ago
September 7
a local apple orchard
September 8
elderly people as grocery baggers, hotel clerks, other jobs
September 9
making wine
September 10
the Battle of Lake Erie won by Oliver Hazard Perry in 1813
September 11
writer's conferences offered in the area
September 12
unusual and historic postcards
September 13
the popularity of the bagel
September 14
fall flowers
September 15
addiction to gambling
September 16
the lottery craze
September 17
Citizenship Day and how it commemorates the signing of the U.S. States Constitution on September 17, 1787

September 18
local tales from elderly people
September 19
dance as therapeutic treatment
September 20
the most chronic back problems and how to avoid them
September 21
restoring old portraits and photographs
September 22
new ways to cook chicken
September 23
sheriff's sales in your county, and how the items for sale are obtained
September 24
dead animals on the road--who disposes of them, and who notifies who that they are there?
September 25
the first newspaper in the American colonies, "Publick Occurrences," that was published in Boston in 1690, and its reception
September 26
weather vanes
September 27
historic Indian relics across the country
September 28
Indian tribes and reservations in your state
September 29
layaway in stores, the average amount of layaway business, whether customers pick up merchandise,

and hard luck stories
September 30
the most popular vacation spots
October 1
how far the automobile industry has come since the Model T Ford made its appearance in 1908
October 2
whether or not keeping a diary is a dying art, and famous published diaries
October 3
originality in applying for a job
October 4
"moonlighting" jobs of law enforcement officers
October 5
whether or not there is really freedom of the press
October 6
successful marriages of handicapped people
October 7
the latest, most enticing chain letters, and whether or not they work
October 8
pyramid type businesses
October 9
the best souvenirs from your city or state
October 10
your local tourist bureau
October 11
jobs that handicapped people hold

October 12
Columbus Day, and since Columbus discovered America in 1492, how many cities bear his name?
October 13
Reminiscences of business leaders in the community, what their fathers wanted them to be, and whether or not they are
October 14
Dwight D. Eisenhower's birthday, and why it is also called National Friendship Day
October 15
the best place in your state to vacation at this time of year
October 16
local mysteries or myths
October 17
excuses given to bill collectors--the most often, the most original
October 18
tough careers (eg: the tax collector, policeman)
October 19
creative part-time jobs for students
October 20
a day with a personal shopper
October 21
limousine services
October 22
unusual names for business and their origins
October 23
creative and unusual jobs of senior citizens

October 24
how United Nations day has been observed since 1945
October 25
the most popular wines, whether wine drinking is increasing or decreasing, and whether wine coolers are replacing wine
October 26
shelters and meals for homeless people in your city
October 27
why the founding of the American Navy occurred in 1775, but Navy Day was not observed until 1922
October 28
how the United States experienced the stock market crash in 1929
October 29
hayriding--historic to present
October 30
scarecrows of today
October 31
Halloween, but also National Magic Day, and Harry Houdini's death in 1926
November 1
modeling as a career for males
November 2
the San Fransicso Bay as discovered by Gaspar de Portola in 1769
November 3
an interview with a male dancer

November 4
Mary Todd's marriage to Abraham Lincoln in 1842, and a comparison of the wedding ceremony to wedding ceremonies of other Presidents

November 5
the latest entertainment and suggestions for office parties

November 6
the craziest bumper stickers

November 7
new products for holiday buying

November 8
where we would be without Wilhelm Rosentgen's discovery of x-rays in 1895

November 9
what is a good deal when buying a car

November 10
how the United States Marine Corps was created in 1775

November 11
how the signing of the armistice ended the war in 1918

November 12
antique clocks and collectors of them

November 13
repossession of cars--how owners lose them and how they are snatched back

November 14
how Nellie Bly set out to circle the globe in less than 80 days

November 15
how motorists and footracers make it to the top of Pike's Peak since it was first sighted by Zebulon Montgomery Pike in 1806

November 16
a local playwright and how he/she gets plots for plays

November 17
a resident of the city who handcrafts jewelry

November 18
the Panama Canal Treaty signed in 1903

November 19
the Gettysburg address given by Abraham Lincoln in 1863, and what it means today

November 20
a female car dealer

November 21
the franchise industry

November 22
President John F. Kennedy's assassination in 1963

November 23
the most rapidly growing city or area in your state

November 24
creative ways for housewives to earn extra money

November 25
the rediscovery of the value of herbs in medicine

November 26
holiday weddings

November 27
Thanksgiving preparations

November 28
the fire at Cocoanut Grove nightclub in Boston that nearly took 500 lives in 1942
November 29
the increase/decrease of shoplifting during the holiday season
November 30
the best cruise deal
December 1
Christmas savings clubs and how they really work
December 2
unusual Christmas greeting cards
December 3
seasonal businesses
December 4
legendary Christmas recipes
December 5
the 21st amendment that was added to the Constitution in 1933 which repealed prohibition
December 6
places to vacation for the holidays
December 7
Pearl Harbor Day (1941) and how it is observed today
December 8
the holiday rush at the Post Office
December 9
suggested gift lists
December 10
using the credit cards for holiday shopping

December 11
special holiday decorations
December 12
the wooden golf tee that was invented in Boston, Massachusetts in 1899, and where we would be without it
December 13
natural gifts (flowers, fruit cake...) for the holidays
December 14
unique gift shops
December 15
popular ski resorts
December 16
how colonists staged the Boston Tea Party in 1773
December 17
handmade gifts
December 18
the latest toys for kids
December 19
the first Christmas message from space by U.S. satellite, Atlas, in 1958 delivered by Dwight D. Eisenhower's radio voice
December 20
how the United States produced electricity from atomic energy for the first time at the Reactor Testing Station in Idaho, 1951
December 21
the pilgrims that stepped ashore at Plymouth Rock in 1620

December 22
various Santa Claus costumes and personalities
December 23
last minute holiday preparations
December 24
Christmas Eve and how it's celebrated by different people
December 25
Christmas Day, and unique celebrations
December 26
the most unusual gifts received
December 27
exchanging and returning gifts
December 28
the post-Christmas blues for businesses
December 29
things to do New Year's Eve
December 30
the fire at Iroquois Theater in Chicago that took 639 lives in 1933
December 31
New Year's resolutions

Conclusion

I'm sure you will find that most of the students in your classes will benefit from most of the writing exercises.

You may notice a difference between writers, particularly on the rewriting and exercises. Surprising enough, you may find that some writers may think that things such as preparing meals and getting dressed are important details, whereas other writers may think these details are less important.

You may find that your students will be so enthusiastic, and contribute in discussions quite spontaneously. Some of the students may become so motivated, that after the sixteen weeks are over, may request private lessons. You could even start a group session with these students or a writers' club.

Thank You!

Made in the USA
San Bernardino, CA
06 September 2017